COPYRIGHT

ISBN 978-1-291-82664-7

CONTENTS

CONTENTS

www.jmguitartuition.co.uk

www.facebook.com/jmguitartuition

Twitter.com/jmguitartuition

www.youtube.com/jmguitartuition

INTRODUCTION

My name is James Martin, and at the time of writing I've played the guitar for the almost two decades – and I've taught others throughout almost all that time.

Over the years, my guitar playing has taken me not only all over my native UK but across the world. I've played in rock bands, blues bands, jazz/funk bands, pop bands, covers bands, originals bands, acoustic trios, duos, solo, orchestras. I've played thrash metal in sweatsoaked clubs and performed classical and flamenco music at weddings and corporate functions.

I've taught thousands of students, from the age of three to those in their seventies, and I've seen my students flourish and find their own voices as fine musicians in their own right. And in that time I've come face to face with how poorly and lazily music is often taught – how many artificial barriers are placed in front of students.

How guitar lessons are often simply an exercise in the "teacher" showing off his own skills. How often music is overcomplicated and the joy and simplicity sapped from it by conventional methods that seem more an exercise in ticking boxes than inspiring creativity.

This book is my attempt to redress the balance - to break down the barriers of jargon and elitism and show you the essential simplicity and elegance of music, and to show that playing music can be a joyful, rewarding and above all intensely personal experience that everyone can be a part of and everyone has a right to share in.

In short, I wrote this book to be the book I wish I'd had when I first picked up the guitar and began my journey - I hope it guides you well on yours.

HOW TO USE THIS BOOK

Music is a universal form of communication that goes deeper into the emotions of the human psyche than language can.

Evolutionary biologists believe that music (in the form of singing) predates language, and this is born out by the sounds of the natural world around us. Birds sing. Dogs bark, and the pitch and tone of their bark conveys joy, fear, aggression or pleading without the need for words.

Rhythm, in its turn, is a vital concept to co-ordinate any kind of group activity, whether orchestra, rock band, dancers or even oarsmen rowing to a beat. Amongst other creatures, humpback whales (a species millions of years older than humanity)have been recognised as using many elements and rules of popular human compositions – rhythms, patterns etc. - in their songs, prompting some

scientists to speculate whether there really is a "universal music" out there awaiting us.

Music has an incredibly powerful effect on the human brain, particularly on the limbic system- an ancient part of the brain that deals with memory formation, as well as emotional and cognitive responses including social functions such as mating.

The discoveries in France and Slovenia of startlingly sophisticated and melodic flute type instruments carved by Neanderthal man from animal bones, dating back a staggering 53,000 years bear this out. Music is an incredibly basic and primal form of communicating emotion that everyone has the ability – and the *right* – to tap into.

Music is NOT something we created. It's something we paid attention to. Remember that.

WHY PLAY THE GUITAR?

All instruments follow the same laws of harmony and melody – all produce the same 12 notes, just in different ways with different tones. For myself, the guitar is the instrument I found I naturally gravitated to, and in a practical sense it has much to recommend it:

The guitar is portable, and highly practical. Ever tried taking a cello on a bus?

The guitar is relatively cheap, simple and robust, particularly Fender-style electrics – Jimi Hendrix was notorious for smashing or setting fire to his guitars to climax his stage shows, but frequently his roadies were able to reconstruct them, bolting the neck from one onto the body of another and putting a fresh set of strings on!

The guitar is very accessible- with a basic feel for rhythm and a few simple chord shapes, it's very easy to accompany yourself or another, or just pick it up and strum along with the radio if a song you happen to like comes on. It's also possible (albeit with more advanced techniques) to produce both a melody and harmony together.

Most importantly, why not? Playing the guitar is a skill that directly rewards effort with achievement, and can bring a real sense of satisfaction to the player as well as entertaining his or her audience. You, the student, are the factor that governs your progress – your efforts will be directly reflected in the results you achieve.

GETTING STARTED

The first and most important thing to remember is, if you want to play guitar, then PLAY it. Pick it up and get stuck in, just make some noise. You don't need rules, you don't need knowledge, you don't need a teacher, hell, *you don't even need this book.*

If you worry about having everything you need before you try playing, you'll never get started – you don't learn to swim by just reading books on it, you learn by putting it into practice, music is the same.

Some of the greatest guitar players of all time started without even having an instrument. The teenage Jimi Hendrix used to wander around playing a broom. The legendary blues guitarist B.B. King taught himself to play slide guitar by nailing one end of a piece of string to the side of his house, nailing the other end into the ground and plucking it while moving a bottle up and down.

Bands like The Beatles and The Rolling Stones got their starts playing skiffle on scavenged and homemade instruments- a tea chest and a broom strung together with wire to form a makeshift bass guitar, washboards pressed into service as percussion instruments etc.

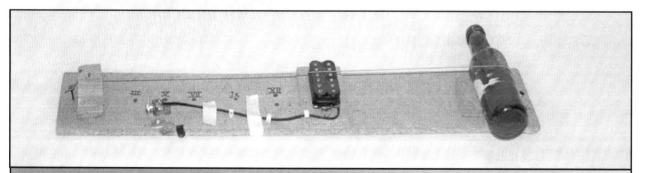

The "Diddly Bow" is a classic example of a primitive home made instrument that many pioneering guitar players got their start on, when guitars were far more expensive in real terms than they are today. The bow is simply a string nailed to a plank of wood at each end, with a bottle lodged underneath to provide resonance. The player beats out a rhythm on the bow and moves a bottle or something similar up and down the string producing varying pitches.

The knowledge and understanding that a good teacher can impart and that this book tries to put across will help you get a better grasp of how music works, can help you approach things in a clear and logical manner and spare the student countless hours of frustration, but it is crucial to realise that these things are nothing without the will of the student to take the initiative and try things for him or her self. It's YOUR guitar and it's there to make the noise YOU want it to make. Other people and other sources of information can help, but they can *only* help, they can't do it for you.

A mantra I repeatedly use with my students is that there are only 12 notes- no matter how complex and impenetrable the song or piece you're trying to play might seem, it was composed and performed by someone with *exactly* the same set of equipment as you – two ears, two eyes, two thumbs, eight fingers. No superpowers. If they can do it, you can too- it's simply a question of time, effort and *practice* - see the box below.

People who claim, "oh, I'm not musical" are simply fulfilling their own prophecy and creating barriers for themselves. I've never met anyone not clinically deaf who can't tell the difference between two notes and that is literally all you need to get started. As I mentioned before, music is simply using pitch and rhythm to communicate on an emotional level, and the ability to recognise this is hardwired into all of us. Play a minor chord to anyone from a native of London, Delhi, Moscow, Tibet, the Amazon jungle – they will all hear and recognise its sad, mournful quality.

Music is a universal currency, something we can all share in experiencing and producing.

A common misconception is that practice is simply a mechanical process- that time spent moving the fingers around will inevitably result in musical ability. Not true. Teaching in schools, I've seen no end of beginner students tell me at the start of the school year, "I've been practicing C all week, Mr Martin", before playing this:

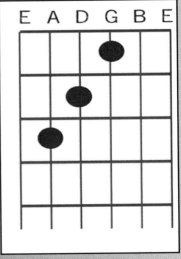

HEAR THIS - AUDIO TRACK 1

Now, let me ask you- does that sound pleasant? Familiar? The kind of thing any sane music teacher would want their student to practice?

Posing that question to the student, I'm usually met with the response "I don't know, I wasn't really listening to it".

Not a *brilliant* attitude for an aspiring musician to take, wouldn't you agree?

So in these instances, the student has been practicing entirely mechanically, paying no attention to the sound they create and as a result the efforts that they've made have been entirely wasted. What they were practicing was NOT the C chord they thought they were practicing and as a result the student has to start all over again - a complete waste of time, resulting in nothing but frustration and disappointment for student and teacher alike.

Practicing is NOT simply a mechanical process, it is a creative one that involves the hands, eyes, ears and above all brain.

Practicing is about trial and error, identifying errors and learning not to make them again, programming shapes and movements into the muscle memory and learning all the many tiny factors that go into creating a pleasing sound- creating something *musical*, however basic the task might seem.

Listening to what you're playing is all important – all too often I've seen guitar players waste their time playing endless runs and exercises that are nothing more than mechanics and having seemingly no regard for the sound that they're creating.

The legendary electric guitar virtuoso Steve Vai offers some fantastic advice to any and all aspiring musicians with these words:

"Stop what you're playing and just listen".

Pick up your guitar. Let's get started.

Thoughts when practicing:

It is better to play one note beautifully than many notes sloppily and carelessly.

You WILL make mistakes - everyone does. Each one is an opportunity to learn and improve.

Strive for perfection in everything you practice.

Listen to, and enjoy, the results.

Whatever you want to learn, you can - it's simply a question of time, patience and concentration.

STAGE 1: BOOT CAMP

GOALS:

In this section of the book you will learn:

— *how to hold the guitar*

— *the parts of the guitar*

— *the names of the strings*

— *how to play in time*

— *how to read tablature*

— *how to produce notes cleanly with both the pick and fret hands*

— *how to play basic single note melodies and riffs*

1A) HOLDING THE GUITAR

It's important to realise from the off that good posture and good technique are all about staying relaxed. Tension and stiffness are the enemies of rhythm and accuracy, and can cause problems later. Musicians are potentially highly vulnerable to conditions like RSI (Repetitive Strain Injury) and Carpal Tunnel Syndrome. A couple of horror stories I've witnessed firsthand- a drummer who insisted on locking his spine and playing absolutely rigidly with his arms and back stiff as a board... suffering back problems by age 25. A classical pianist whose teacher had always instructed her to sit absolutely straight up and rigid – arthritis in the shoulders by age 30.

Don't let this put you off though, because these issues are actually very easy to avoid with the application of just a modicum of common sense. First, and most importantly, if whatever you're doing starts to hurt, then *just stop doing it!* Learning the guitar involves programming many new movements into your muscle memory, utilising the joints and the fingers in new and unfamiliar ways. Trying to force too much too soon will lead to pain, stiffness and ultimately impede your development- pain is there for a reason, it's your body telling you that you're doing it damage, respect those signals.

"I bought my first real six string / played it till my fingers bled" - yes, thank you Mr. Bryan Adams, and you then had to spend the next couple of weeks in pain while your fingertips healed and scarred over to the point where you could play again, by which point you'd forgotten everything you'd learned and had to start over from scratch again. Left that bit out, didn't you?

Firstly then, let's consider posture. Whether you choose to sit or stand with the guitar, it's important to try and avoid hunching over to peer at what you're doing, as doing this repeatedly for long periods of time can cause lower back pain. For those who choose to sit, I'd recommend placing the guitar over the right thigh and if you need to look at the fretboard, angle the guitar neck back slightly as this will prevent you from having to hunch yourself over.

For those who prefer to stand, the first thing to do is to set the strap height – yes, down by the knees Slash/ Jimmy Page style may look cool, but if you're just starting out you're going to find it makes things much more difficult than they have to be. Adjust the strap to roughly waist height, check that you can comfortably see and access the entire fretboard without having to twist yourself round and then adjust to comfort from there.

Whether sat or stood, it's important to stay relaxed, not to have to stretch or hunch or put any additional stress through your shoulders, back and wrists. Relax - you'll play longer!

At all times the guitar should sit comfortably in your lap or with the strap across your shoulder with the weight spread evenly and with no need for excessive effort to see and access the fretboard.

Now, onto the unsung hero of the fretting hand – the thumb. Finding the right thumb position for you is critical to being able to play cleanly, and (I can't emphasise this enough) it can *only* be found by the student through trial and error. Every student is different, and every student needs to put the time in to find where their thumb should sit to play the notes cleanly and avoid any unnecessary stress being placed on their joints and wrist.

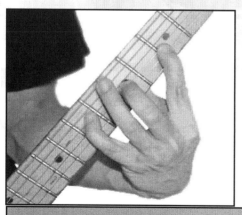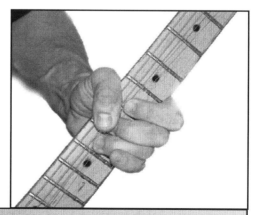

Thumb behind the neck (left) this is the technique prescribed in classical guitar, as it allows the hand to reach it's maximum span, allowing for clear fretting of chord arpeggios and also wide stretch legato playing.

Thumb over the neck (right) - most blues and rock players use this type of technique as it helps with bending and vibrato.

1A) HOLDING THE GUITAR CONT.

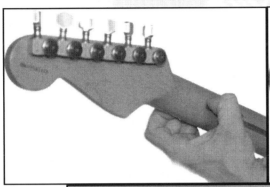 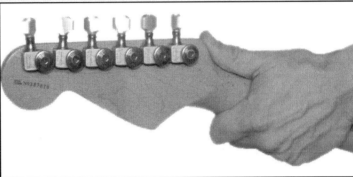

Some illustrations of what not to do- particularly try and avoid anything that places any stress through the thumb or the wrist as this will prevent your fingers from moving fluidly and can cause issues with your wrists down the line.

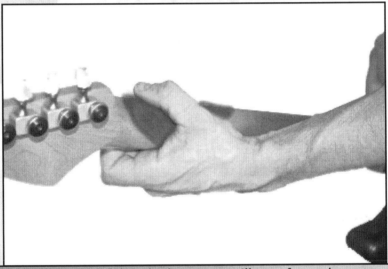

Although the exact details of thumb placement will vary from player to player and guitar to guitar, for most people the most comfortable place will be in the shaded area indicated.

Put simply, what's right is what works and doesn't hurt- good thumb technique and posture will enable the player to stay relaxed and play for hours without causing any aches, pains or stiffness.

Now that you've got comfortable holding the instrument, let's move on to playing it...

1B) ANATOMY OF THE GUITAR

Guitars are relatively simple instruments - certainly, as electric guitar players, we're generally playing evolutions of instruments designed in the 1950s, while the history of the acoustic guitar traces its lineage all the way back to the medieval lute - but they do have a few component parts and it's useful to know what these are .

After all, it's all very well being told to use the bridge pickup, or hold your pick closer to the sound hole, but unless you the student know what these things are, it's not going to be very edifying!

So, for reference, here is a quick guide to what's what and where on the guitar-

FIG 1) THE ELECTRIC GUITAR

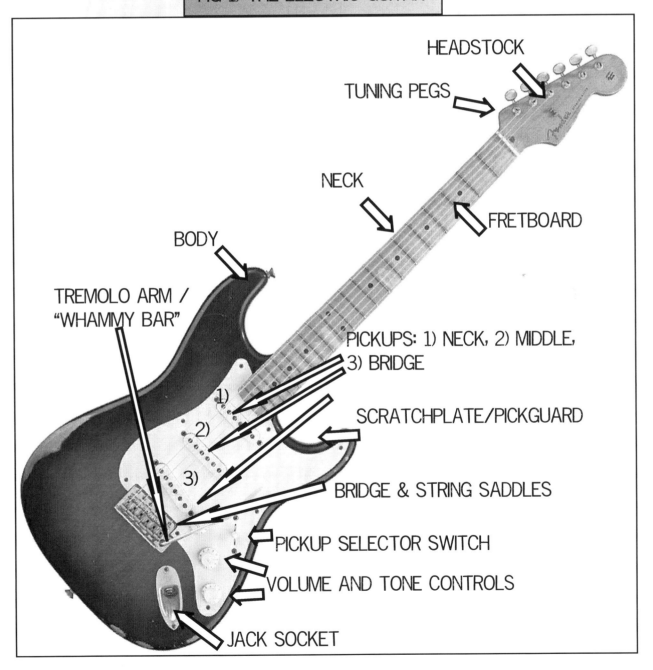

HEADSTOCK

TUNING PEGS

NECK

FRETBOARD

BODY

TREMOLO ARM / "WHAMMY BAR"

PICKUPS: 1) NECK, 2) MIDDLE, 3) BRIDGE

1)

2)

3)

SCRATCHPLATE/PICKGUARD

BRIDGE & STRING SADDLES

PICKUP SELECTOR SWITCH

VOLUME AND TONE CONTROLS

JACK SOCKET

Don't worry - it may look complicated, but it becomes second nature very quickly. Also, nobody's expecting you to memorise this stuff, so feel free to look at this guide again!

1B) ANATOMY OF THE GUITAR CONT.

Although electric guitars usually have an array of controls to help shape their sound, acoustic guitars (whether nylon or steel strung) all work pretty much the same way, using the resonance of the guitar body to amplify the vibrations of the strings. As with electric guitars, there are many different types of woods used in the construction and the choice of wood can have a major impact on the tone of the guitar, as can the size and shape of the body itself.

FIG 2) THE ACOUSTIC GUITAR

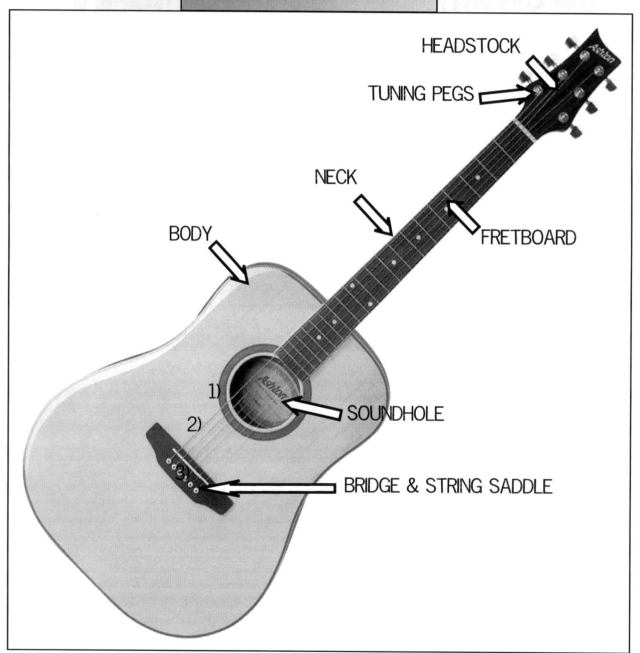

HEADSTOCK

TUNING PEGS

NECK

FRETBOARD

BODY

1)

2)

SOUNDHOLE

BRIDGE & STRING SADDLE

Acoustic guitars are sometimes fitted with a pickup to allow them to be amplified further. These electro-acoustic guitars still look, play and sound like acoustic guitars, but have the option of being plugged into an amplifier or PA to enable them to be played with a band.

1C) TUNING THE GUITAR

Each string is tuned to a different note - on a conventional sis string acoustic or electric guitar, these notes are (low to high) -E, A, D, G, B, E

There's an easy way to remember this - a simple mnemonic that goes like this:

Eric Ate Dynamite, Good Bye Eric

Now, convention has it that we refer to the strings as "high" or "low" based on the sound that they produce.

However, this has the unfortunate and slightly confusing situation whereby the thin E string, the one closest to the floor, is referred to as the "high" E, whilst the one closest to the ceiling is the "low" E...

Welcome to the wonderful world of guitar where high is low and low is high, and to make it even more confusing, they're both named E....

It gets easier. Trust me.

FIG 2) OPEN STRING TUNING NOTES, LOW E - HIGH E

FIG 3) THE STRING NAMES

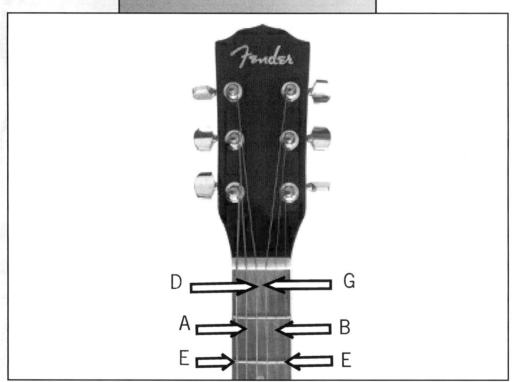

This is known as standard, or occasionally "Spanish" tuning, which is what we'll be using throughout this book.

There are, however, a wide variety of alternate tunings popular on the guitar:

"Slack" tuning - everything down a semitone - Eb, Ab, Db, Gb, Bb, Eb

"Drop D" - D, A,D, G, B, E

Open tunings (where the guitar is tuned to a chord) -

Open G - D, G, D, G, B, D   Open E - E, B, E, G#, B, E

"DADGAD" - D, A, D, G, A, D

1D) RHYTHM

Some years ago, one of my students asked me what made music *music*, as opposed to simply random noise. This was a very interesting question, as all too often it's easy to get caught up in the details, the "how", and lose touch with what it is we're trying to accomplish. We discussed this question at some length, and came to the conclusion that rhythm was the answer - without rhythm, music becomes entirely random and unpredictable, and the human brain abhors randomness.

Rhythm helps us to feel the patterns in a piece of music, helps us to understand and predict what will happen next - and deciphering those patterns, successfully making those predictions and seeing them fulfilled is what releases dopamine, the "feel-good" chemical which stimulates the pleasure centres in the brain.

So, no, Groove Is NOT In The Heart, it's in the Mind...

Thinking about this a little more deeply, you can come to realise that rhythm is an essential part of a staggering number of activities- how many times have you heard athletes talk about finding the "groove" of the game or track? In ancient times, armies trained to the beat of drums, and navies used drummers to ensure their rowers coordinated their efforts effectively. In hospitals today, when using ECT treatment to revive a patient, it is essential for the operator to be able to feel the rhythm of a pulse in order to predict when to apply the current. For any group activity, for the participants to be properly coordinated, there is an underlying rhythm present- from an orchestra to a football team to a pack of wolves stalking their prey.

So those who say they have no sense of rhythm are over-thinking the problem, rhythm is a natural instinct. I'll prove it. With your thumb over the veins in your wrist or your neck, clear your mind and feel your heart beating. As you feel the regularity of the rhythm, as your heart pumps out it's on beat, start to tap your foot or nod your head gently to your body's own rhythm. THAT is your own internal metronome. A song has a pulse, just like any living thing - find your pulse, listen to it and match it as closely as you can.

The speed of the pulse is known as the *tempo* of the song. The tempo can be fast or slow, but it is almost always **consistent** (*almost* – a notable exception is Led Zeppelin's classic "Stairway To Heaven" which gradually builds pace and momentum throughout). If you're going to play a song and have it sound like a song, like a complete and coherent musical entity, having a solid and consistent tempo is an absolute must.

We'll begin with a very simple exercise to get the rhythmic juices flowing.

If you have a metronome or drum machine, now is the time to use it – if not, use the one provided in the audio accompaniment or simply tap your foot (for most people, tapping their feet to a song is a simple and natural reaction to rhythm- the foot is used to tapping along to a beat, so use it to guide your picking hand. As the foot taps the beat, the pick hand strikes the string at the same time.).

We'll begin by playing each open string, low to high, along with the beat, and your goal is to play each note exactly on the beat as demonstrated in the audio accompaniment.

Time to make some noise.

1D) RHYTHM

HOW TO READ NOTATION: TAB

Reading music is an intimidating prospect for a beginner on any instrument, struggling to master unfamiliar patterns and techniques, to control the fingers while they learn to perform awkward and often seemingly impossible contortions. Start adding in trying to decipher the bizarre and incomprehensible hieroglyphics and the challenge starts to seem insurmountable!

Happily, we guitarists have developed an easy-to-read alternative to traditional music notation in the form of tablature, or "tab" for short. Over the last few decades this system has become effectively the standard for guitarists (and bassists, and banjo players) who deal primarily with popular styles.

Tablature dates from around 1300 and has long been an alternative to standard notation for players of fretted stringed instruments such as the lute (the medieval precursor to the guitar) vihuela (an early guitar-like instrument with paired strings similar to the modern day twelve-string) or mandolin.

Modern day tablature represents the strings of the guitar going from the low E to the high E as horizontal lines, and the numbers of the frets to be played written on them . The number "0", zero, is used to denote an open string (ie, one played without any notes fretted.)

EXAMPLE

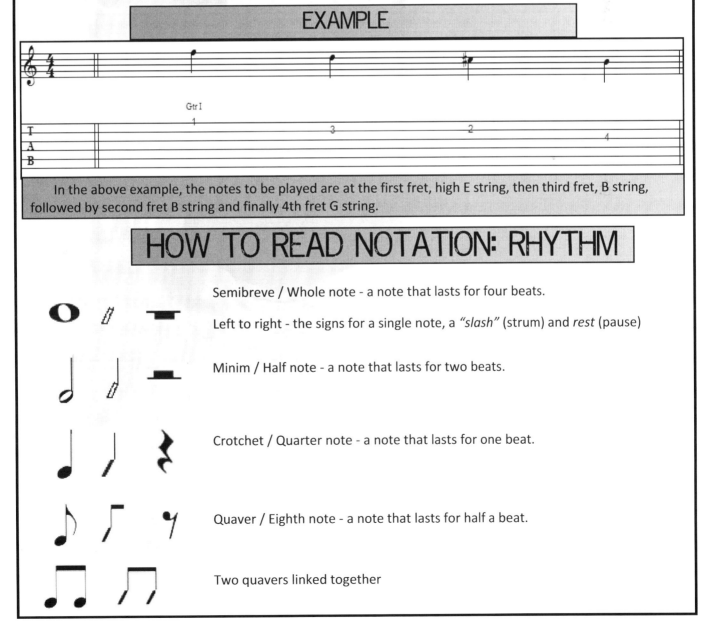

In the above example, the notes to be played are at the first fret, high E string, then third fret, B string, followed by second fret B string and finally 4th fret G string.

HOW TO READ NOTATION: RHYTHM

Semibreve / Whole note - a note that lasts for four beats.

Left to right - the signs for a single note, a *"slash"* (strum) and *rest* (pause)

Minim / Half note - a note that lasts for two beats.

Crotchet / Quarter note - a note that lasts for one beat.

Quaver / Eighth note - a note that lasts for half a beat.

Two quavers linked together

1D) RHYTHM cont. / !E) FRETTING

EX 1A) OPEN STRINGS (AUDIO TRACK 3) - BACKING TRACK (AUDIO TRACK 4)

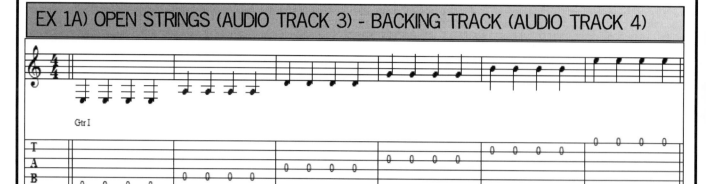

Your aim is to play these notes as closely in time with the drum backing as possible. Once you've mastered this exercise as demonstrated and written out here, try turning the pattern around and playing it backwards.

What we've played here is known as **crotchet** or **quarter-note** rhythm - playing one note on each beat. Now let's try and mix that up a little and add in some activity from the fret hand.

EX 1B) THE SPIDER (AUDIO TRACK 5) - BACKING TRACK (AUDIO TRACK 6)

*This exercise is played out of **first position** and trains the fret hand in **"one finger one fret"** technique – simply put, this means that we begin with the first finger at the first fret, and behind that the other fingers fall into place- second finger deals with the second fret, third finger third fret, and little finger with the fourth fret. In order to play smoothly and well, each finger has a job to do and needs to be trained to do that job- the goal of this exercise is to synchronise the picking and fretting hands so that each note is played cleanly, and to ensure that each finger is activated.*

Having played the pattern ascending from low to high E strings, we'll now turn that pattern around and play it backwards (a technique known in music jargon as **retrograde**). This will probably feel rather disorientating at first, as you'll be leading off with the little finger or pinky, which is the smallest, weakest and laziest of the fingers.

EX 1C) REVERSE SPIDER (AUDIO TRACK 7) - BACKING TRACK (AUDIO TRACK 8)

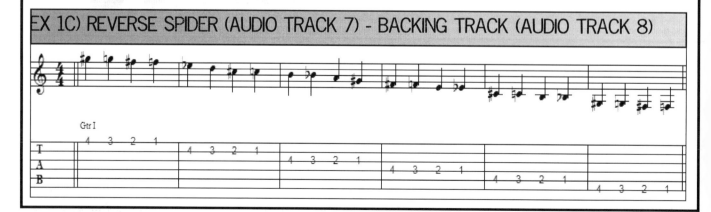

1E) FRETTING CONT.

Now, this may sound like I have a grudge against the little finger, but actually it's simple biology- very few activities tend to engage the little finger (with the exception of specialised techniques such as sign language or touch typing), so the neural pathways - literally, the connections through which commands and sensations are passed between the brain and little finger are rusty and underused.

To put it another way, if the neural pathways to the first and second fingers are like smooth gleaming motorways free from traffic, the pathway to the little finger is usually a dirt track overgrown with brambles and thorns.. However, to play the guitar well, we'll need all four fingers (and occasionally the thumb) firing on all cylinders, so work that pinky!

JARGON BUSTER - *FIRST POSITION*

First position means the first finger takes position at the first fret and is responsible for all the notes played at that fret. The second finger, in its turn, deals with the notes at the second fret, third finger takes care of the third fret and little finger takes care of the fourth fret.

Second position moves everything up a fret - first finger takes care of the second fret, second finger takes care of the third, and so on.

JARGON BUSTER - *ONE FINGER ONE FRET*

This is pretty much exactly what it sounds like - each finger is assigned to a fret, so for example if the hand is in fifth position, the first finger would take care of the fifth fret, second finger sixth fret, third finger seventh fret and little finger eighth fret . One-finger-one-fret playing is one of the basic fundamental principles of good technique.

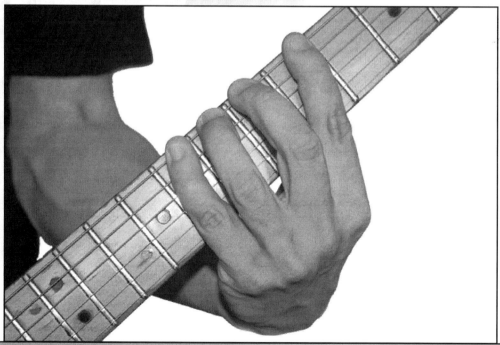

This picture demonstrates the one-finger, one-fret idea perfectly - here the hand is in fifth position, the first finger is fretting the fifth fret, second, the sixth and so on.

Programming this approach into your fingers will ensure that you always instinctively know which finger to use to play a note, thus enabling you to play faster, more fluidly and more accurately.

1E) FRETTING CONT.

Now, with our newfound dexterity, let's put those fingers to work playing some simple single- note *riffs*.

Riffs are a staple of rock, blues, metal and pretty much every style of popular music and are an easy and fun way to get started. Those of you with experience reading music will find the notation easy to follow, those of you who haven't (most of the people reading this book will fall into this category), don't worry about the notation, simply follow the tab and use your ear to help pick out the rhythm.

Check out the notes that go with each riff for fingerings to use.

I've tabbed out several simple riffs in the style of some of the all time rock classics , so get stuck in and have some fun with them. When you've mastered these riffs, try tweaking them - changing the rhythm here, adding or changing a note there - and see what you can come up with on your own.

The guitar has a wonderful tradition of improvising and experimenting, so don't be afraid to try out your own ideas - if you like it, odds are someone else will too!

JARGON BUSTER - *RIFF*

A riff is musical slang, short for a *repeating figure* – a phrase or motif that repeats throughout the song and "hooks" the listener in, almost like a song within a song.

Often it is the part of the song that we think of first and recognise most easily – think of classic riffs like Deep Purple's "Smoke On The Water", Led Zeppelin's "Whole Lotta Love" or "Satisfaction" by The Rolling Stones.

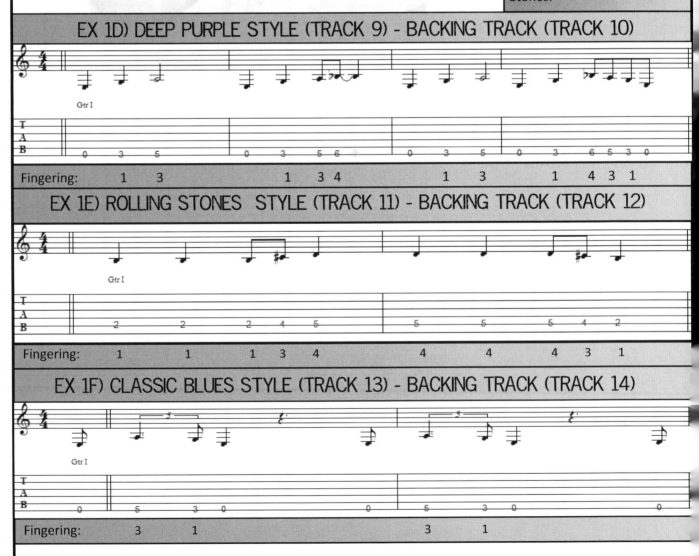

EX 1D) DEEP PURPLE STYLE (TRACK 9) - BACKING TRACK (TRACK 10)

EX 1E) ROLLING STONES STYLE (TRACK 11) - BACKING TRACK (TRACK 12)

EX 1F) CLASSIC BLUES STYLE (TRACK 13) - BACKING TRACK (TRACK 14)

BOOT CAMP SUMMARY

IN THIS SECTION, YOU HAVE LEARNED:

— *how to hold the guitar*

— *the parts of the guitar*

— *the names of the strings*

— *how to play in time*

-*how to read tablature*

— *how to produce notes cleanly with both the pick and fret hands*

— *how to play basic single note melodies and riffs*

BOOT CAMP PRACTICE ROUTINE

10-15 minutes per day, 7 - 14 days depending on the student.

1) Warm up - open strings played in time *(3- 5 minutes)*

2) Spider exercise - 1st position, and then variations when mastered- variation examples below *(3-5 minutes)*

3) Riffs - master them as written and recorded and then experiment! Try varying the rhythm ,varying the notes, playing them in different positions etc. - most importantly, have fun with them! *(4-5 minutes)*

STAGE 2: FIRST STEPS

GOALS:

In this section of the book you will learn

— what a chord is

— the five crucial chord shapes that underpin everything on the fretboard

— basic strumming and accompaniment techniques

— how to practice effectively

— what the 12 bar blues is, its importance in popular music, and how to play it

2A) WHAT IS A CHORD?

A chord is the musical term for a group of notes that, when played together, produce a particular mood or feel. Chords are a great way of easily creating a full and musical sound on the guitar without requiring much in the way of experience or technique.

We can think of music as having three basic elements to it - the **melody** (tune), generally played by a lead instrument or sung.

Beneath that, there is the **rhythm,** the beat that keeps everything together and moving in time. We dealt with the fundamentals of rhythm in the Boot Camp section, but there will be more on that to come in this section.

In between rhythm and supporting the melody comes the harmony, filling the space between melody and rhythm and providing a bed of sound for the melody to be laid upon. Think about it for a moment - how many of your favourite songs would sound empty if it was simply a melody and a drumbeat? This is where chords come in, and as guitar players, we will spend most of our time playing supporting chordal parts in one way or another.

I've been asked before by students how many chords there are, and I think the truth is that there are an almost infinite variety of ways to sculpt notes into harmonies that reflect the subtleties of human emotions. There are always new chords to be found - and new ways of playing familiar chords.

Major (music jargon for "happy sounding") chords are the default type of chord, so for example a G major chord will simply be written and referred to as a G. You can always assume you're playing a major chord unless otherwise specified!

There are literally tens of thousands of possible chord combinations and shapes – I've seen, and you may well also have, chord dictionaries in your local music store boasting 10,000 or 20,000 different chord shapes in their pages, and it's very easy to feel incredibly intimidated by the idea that you have to commit all these shapes to memory simply in order to get started.

So, good news …

…yeah, you don't have to do that.

At all.

In fact, that attitude of rote learning is tedious, inefficient, ineffective and sometimes downright harmful to the student trying to gain a fundamental understanding of the guitar. There are some constants and reference points that you do need to memorise, but they are very, very few in number.

The simple truth is, everything you play on the guitar can be related back to a mere five simple chord shapes. With these five shapes and the twelve notes of the chromatic scale (more on that later), you can conquer the world..

Or the guitar fretboard, at the very least.

2B) THE BIG FIVE CHORDS - THE CAGED SYSTEM

The CAGED system is, quite simply, the basic manual for how the guitar fretboard works.

The system revolves around the fact that the guitar fretboard can be split down into five different chord shapes - C, A, G, E and D. All other chords, no matter how sophisticated and complex sounding, can be related back to one of these five shapes.

Riffs, melodies and scale patterns can also be related back to these five shapes - so being able to master them is a crucial first step to mastering the guitar itself.

So, let's get started:

THE C CHORD (TRACK 15)

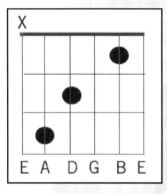
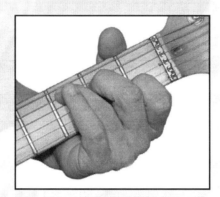
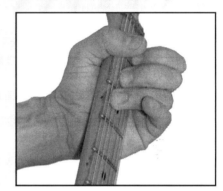

Here is the C chord shape depicted in a grid - this tells you to place your first finger on the first fret, B string, second finger on the second fret, D string, and third finger on the third fret, A string.

Arch your fingers so that only the tips are in contact with the strings and strum from the A string down towards the floor.

Here I've shown the shapes your fingers should form: *(left)* if looking at your fingers in a mirror and *(right)* looking down the fretboard at your fingers.

Finally, here is the C chord written both in standard music notation and in tablature.

To hear the C chord played with a strum motion and as an *arpeggio,* play Track 15

JARGON BUSTER - *ARPEGGIO*

An *arpeggio* is simply a bit of flash musical terminology for a chord played one note at a time, so in this instance we can *arpeggiate* the chord by picking one string at a time. This is useful to check that each note within the chord shape is cleanly fretted and rings out true. Remember the importance of adjusting your thumb position if you find you struggle with muted notes.

2B) THE BIG FIVE CHORDS - THE CAGED SYSTEM

THE G CHORD (TRACK 16)

E A D G B E

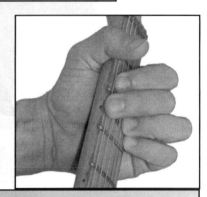

(left) the G chord *(right)* the G chord as seen looking down the fretboard

Here is the G chord shape depicted in a grid - this tells you to place your first finger on the second fret, A string, second finger on the third fret, low E string, and third finger on the third fret, high E string.

Strum all six strings for the G.

Finally, here is the G chord written both in standard music notation and in tablature.

Note the two different fingerings - both are equally fine to use, it's down to personal taste.

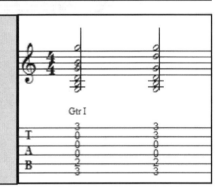

THE D CHORD (TRACK 17)

X X

E A D G B E

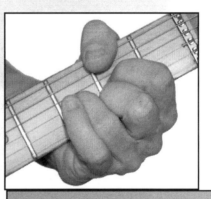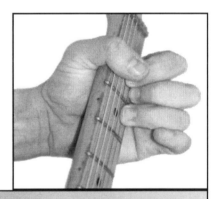

(left) the D chord *(right)* the D chord as seen looking down the fretboard

Here is the D chord grid - this tells you to place your first finger on the second fret, G string, second finger on the second fret, high E string, and third finger on the third fret, B string.

Strum all from the D string downwards - watch your picking hand with the D!

...And here is the D chord written both in standard music notation and in tablature.

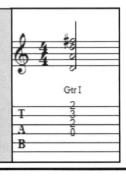

2B) THE BIG FIVE CHORDS - THE CAGED SYSTEM

THE A CHORD (TRACK 18)

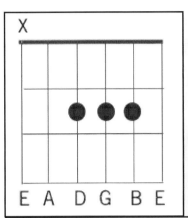

X

E A D G B E

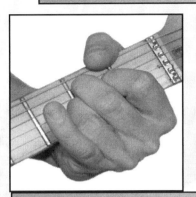

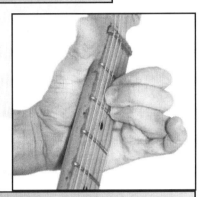

(left) the A chord *(right)* the A chord as seen looking down the fretboard.

Notice the two different fingerings illustrated - choose whichever works best for you.

Here is the A chord shape depicted in a grid - notice that you need to fret the same second fret on the D, G and B strings. You may have to experiment with fingering and thumb positioning to get this chord cleanly.

Strum from the A string downward for this chord.

Finally, here is the A chord written both in standard music notation and in tablature.

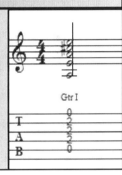

THE E CHORD (TRACK 19)

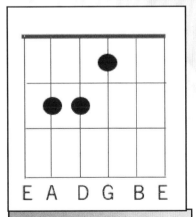

E A D G B E

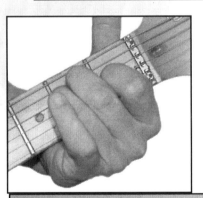

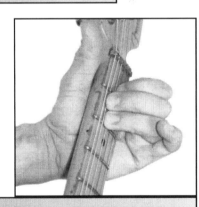

(left) the E chord *(right)* the E chord as seen looking down the fretboard

Here is the E chord grid - this tells you to place your first finger on the first fret, G string, second finger on the second fret, A string, and third finger on the second fret, D string.

Strum all six strings for the E chord.

...And here is the E chord written both in standard music notation and in tablature.

2C) STRUMMING PATTERNS AND FIRST SONGS

WHOLE NOTE (SEMIBREVE) STRUMMING (TRACK 20)

Here I'm playing each chord once every four beats. This rhythm is known as a *whole note* or *semibreve* rhythm, and is written like so:

Ex 1:

Count: "one   two   three   four / one   two   three   four"

Try this with each chord in turn. When you've got the hang of it, move on to....

HALF NOTE (MINIM) STRUMMING (TRACK 21)

With this rhythm, I'm playing each chord once every two beats. This rhythm is known as a *half note* or *minim* rhythm, and is written like so:

Ex 2:

Count: "one   two   three   four / one   two   three   four"

Note that it seems faster even though the speed of the beat hasn't changed - we're just playing more chords in the same space.

Again, try this with each chord in turn. When you've got the hang of it, move on to....

QUARTER NOTE (CROTCHET) STRUMMING (TRACK 22)

Finally, here, I'm playing the chord once on every beat. This rhythm is known as a *quarter note* or *crotchet* rhythm, and is written like so:

Ex 3:

Count: "one   two   three   four / one   two   three   four"

Again, it seems faster even though the speed of the beat hasn't changed - we're just playing more chords in the same space, playing a chord every beat instead of waiting for two or four beats.

Notice also that we're grouping these beats into sets of four. These are known as bars, and a re a very important and useful musical concept.

JARGON BUSTER - *BARS*

As you've already seen, we keep track of the progress of a piece of music by counting the beats. Now, as most songs tend to be based on repeating patterns of chords, it makes things far easier to group these beats together into sets known as *bars* - what's easier, counting 4 bars or sixteen beats?

The number of beats per bar is known as the time signature - for most of the songs we'll be dealing with, we'll be using the commonest time signature of all, 4/4 , which means four crotchet beats to the bar. This underpins pretty much all standard rock and pop material.

2C) STRUMMING PATTERNS AND FIRST SONGS

Now, we're going to start stringing these chords together to form whole songs. Each song will use the *crotchet* or *quarter note* rhythm covered in the previous page.

Knocking On My Old Front Door

// G D / C //

If you've never seen a chord chart before, let me explain - this is a very quick and simple way to jot down the basic harmony of a song and share it with band members, so chart reading is a useful and easy skill to acquire.

The double slashes ("**//**" symbol) denote the start and end of the piece. The single slash separates the piece out into *bars* (see p.22 Jargon Buster for an explanation on this).

In the absence of anything telling us differently, we can assume that the piece is in 4/4 - that is, four crotchet beats to the bar (again, see p.22 Jargon Buster for an explanation on this).

In the first bar, we have two chords - half a bar (two beats) of G, half a bar (two beats) of D - and then a whole bar (4 beats) of C to follow. Played at a constant tempo we should have the following:

Count:	"one	two	three	four /	one	two	three	four"
Chord:	G	G	D	D /	C	C	C	C

KNOCKING ON MY OLD FRONT DOOR   (TRACK 23)

BACKING TRACK (TRACK 24)

Let's try this with a few other chord combinations:

Fortuitous Man - // G D / A //

FORTUITOUS MAN - TRACK 25, BACKING TRACK - TRACK 26

Sweet Home Kentucky - // D C / G //

SWEET HOME KENTUCKY - TRACK 27, BACKING TRACK - TRACK 28

Hatful Of Coconut - // E D / A //

HATFUL OF COCONUT- TRACK 29, BACKING TRACK - TRACK 30

Hey Jimi - // C G / D A / E / E //

HEY JIMI- TRACK 31, BACKING TRACK - TRACK 32

2C) STRUMMING PATTERNS AND FIRST SONGS

HOW TO PRACTICE: PREPARATION AND PERFORMANCE

When you're playing a song, you are *committed*. It's almost like walking a tightrope- once you're on that tightrope, you don't get to stop, you have to just follow through to the end. Your balance may wobble, you may have to steady yourself but the most important thing is to follow that tightrope to the end!

It is inevitable that as a guitarist you will make mistakes, you will fumble some notes and some chord changes. However, just as it is important to practice not making those mistakes, it is also equally important to practice not letting those mistakes throw you! For this reason it is important to draw a distinction between the *preparation* and *performance* aspects of practicing.
For example, here's how we might go about applying this to the next song, the 12 bar blues in G. We'll start with preparation, looking at the individual ingredients for the song.

First, we isolate the chord shapes- we're going to need G, C & D to play this. So we practice them in isolation, arpeggiating each shape, ensuring that our fingers can wrap themselves around the basic elements of the song.

Next, we start practicing them in the order we'll need them for the song- in this case, that's G, C, G, D, C, G, D. Just arpeggiate the chords in that order, there's no need to worry about counting beats or bars quite yet. Your fingers are still learning the shapes, and crucially, mapping out the moves necessary to change form chord to chord.

Once we've successfully dealt with that stage, we can look at the rhythms we're going to be using and practice any of them in isolation. As it is, for this song we'll be using a simple crotchet rhythm (i.e. one per beat) so we can probably skip this stage.

So, with preparation dealt with, let's move on to performance. Now, I'm going to come right out and say this- you're almost certain to go wrong somewhere in this song. Whether it's a finger in the wrong place or a missed strum, the reality is it's not going to be perfect.

And that's absolutely fine. The important thing is to play *all* the song, with a consistent steady pulse behind it. Don't try and go back to correct a mistake. You're trying, as far as possible, to kid your audience into believing it was intentional in the first place!

Once you've finished, evaluate your performance. Any mistakes? Yes? Then let's isolate those mistakes, go back to *preparation* mode, see if we can iron them out. With that done, let's try performing the song again. The extra preparation should give you the confidence to anticipate any mistakes and also knowing that you've practiced the tricky bits means you'll be more relaxed about playing them- and therefore less likely to go wrong.

And that, in a nutshell, is the most efficient approach to practicing. A good analogy is with motor racing. Most race meetings are divided into three stages - practice, qualifying and race day. Practice and qualifying are where the drivers learn the track and try to prepare themselves for any eventualities- this is analogous to the *preparation* side of practice, i.e. picking and strumming through the chords, practicing any tricky changes or time counts.

Come race day, however, it's foot down and go for it. And that's the same for us. Play the song, finish the song, keep the rhythm and the groove even if your fingers might occasionally might end up in the wrong place!

How To Practice Efficiently

When you're happy with all the individual elements, then go to:

Assess performance:
Isolate and identify problem areas.

Return to:

Preparation

Performance

Prepare each individual element:

Programme chord shapes and changes into fingers, isolate and work out any tricky fingerings
Count / tap / strum rhythm patterns

Practice perfection of "form" and execution

Strive for rhythm , pulse, groove - above all CONTINUITY.

Stay on the tightrope and finish the song, even if you make mistakes.

THE IMPORTANCE OF FOCUS

As students of the guitar- or indeed any musical instrument - we are often told that "practice makes perfect". But this is really only half the story. A truer statement would be that you will only get out of a practice session what you put into it. Two minutes spent intensely practicing a technical weak spot or a persistent problem area within a song is immensely more valuable than an hour spent vaguely strumming with one eye on the TV and an ear not concentrating on the sound produced.

Consider two beginner students, both given the same task- in their respective lessons, they have both learned the chord shapes G, D and C. Their homework, over the week, is to familiarise themselves with these shapes to the point where they can play them perfectly and consistently so that in the next lesson we can use these shapes to start playing some basic songs (Knocking On Heaven's Door, Sweet Home Alabama, Sweet Child O'Mine- all use these simple chord shapes).

The first student follows the practice routine diligently- he starts with the chromatic "spider" warm up exercise, playing slowly and carefully, taking care to line up each note perfectly before playing it. He then goes through each of the chord shapes one by one, arpeggiating each one and taking care to adjust his thumb to find the "sweet spot" where the notes ring out. There are muted notes and clicks, but he perseveres- no one else is going to get it right for him, are they? By this point he's been practicing for about 10 minutes, so spends a couple of minutes practicing basic strumming patterns (whole notes/semibreves, half notes/minims, quarter notes/crotchets) and then winds down with that old staple, "Smoke On The Water"- he knows it well, knows he can play it and have it sound recognisable, so he finishes the 15 minute practice session with a positive feeling, looking forward to playing again tomorrow.

THE IMPORTANCE OF FOCUS CONT.

By the third or fourth day the spider exercise is getting quicker and more accurate, and the chord shapes are becoming more consistent as the student can recognise patterns and shapes amongst the chord shapes- the C resembling a curve with an "open window" on the G string, the D resembling a pyramid or triangle pointing up the fretboard toward the body of the guitar- so the student starts to string them together, slowly at first, and notices how some changes remind him of songs he knows well.

By the time the next lesson has come round, the student's "Spider" warm up exercise is more controlled and accurate (although still slow, which is fine- speed is NOT the goal here) and the three chords are clear and secure, as are the three basic rhythms. As a result, we can start to combine them in different ways to start playing some actual songs, albeit in slightly simplified fashion. Over the next week, the student starts to add these songs to his repertoire, and also feels confident enough to start experimenting with alterations to the chords and combining them in different ways to some up with his own ideas.

The second student skips out the "Spider" warm up as he finds it boring and decides to go straight to the chords. He lines up the chord shapes and strums them listlessly while browsing the Net or watching TV, not really listening to or engaging with the results. His fingers don't learn to grasp the sweet spots on the fretboard to have the notes ring out cleanly and his chords are muffled and muted. However, he figures he's putting his fingers in roughly the right places and he can call the time he's spent "practice" so he thinks he's done his homework.

Come his next lesson, his "Spider" warm up is sloppy and messy, muted notes and incorrect strings ringing out everywhere, his chords are full of basic errors, sounding muffled and muted and hideously unmusical and the entire lesson has to be devoted to redoing the same topics as the previous week. Result- zero progress for the student. "But I practiced for almost an hour every night" the student protests....

The moral of this story is pretty clear – practice WILL bring results. But it will ONLY bring them if you are fully engaged with what you're doing, eyes, ears, fingers and brain all working together to shape the sound and create something musical. Patience and concentration is an absolute must, as it is when you are learning any sort of craft or skill, and it is astonishing how many students fail to recognise this, condemning themselves (and their poor teacher!) to frustration. Think about learning to drive – what would happen if you failed to pay attention to the road? Think about someone learning to paint without bothering to look at what they're painting, or someone trying to master a martial art without concentrating on balance, movement etc.

You will only get from practice what you put into it in the first place in terms of focus, concentration and awareness. Fifteen minutes of practice, fully engaged with every aspect of what you're doing, beats out two hours of mindless strumming any day of the week. It's not about marking time, it's about results.

The medicine works. But it will only work if you take it.

2D) THE 12 BAR BLUES

The 12 bar blues pattern is an absolutely crucial idea to master. It's a pattern that sits right at the heart of a huge amount of pop and rock music, and one that no guitar player should be without.

WHAT IS THE TWELVE BAR BLUES?

WHY IS IT IMPORTANT?

The twelve bar blues is a pattern of chord changes that underpins literally tens of thousands of different songs. As well as the blues genre itself, this pattern is also at the heart of rock 'n' roll, country music, and to a lesser extent jazz, soul and pop music.

For example, if you've ever listened to much in the way of blues or old rock 'n' roll music such as Jerry Lee Lewis, Chuck Berry etc., you may have noticed a surprising degree of similarity between many of the songs. This is because very often they follow the same pattern of chord changes, simply with different rhythms, arrangements, melodies and lyrics. The versatility of the 12 bar blues allows it to be used for many different types of songs. Some examples include:

BLUES	ROCK 'N' ROLL	SOUL / JAZZ / COUNTRY	POP/ ROCK
The Thrill Is Gone (B.B. King)	Johnny B. Goode (Chuck Berry)	Mustang Sally (Otis Redding)	Mercy (Duffy)
Red House (Jimi Hendrix)	Route 66 (The Rolling Stones)	What'd I Say (Ray Charles)	One Room Paradise (Aretha Franklin - re-recorded by Elayna Boynton)
Love Struck Baby (Stevie Ray Vaughan)	Shake, Rattle & Roll (Big Joe Turner)	Folsom Prison Blues (Johnny Cash)	Give Me One Reason (Tracy Chapman)
Stop Breaking Down (Robert Johnson - covered by The Rolling Stones)	Rock Around The Clock (Bill Haley & The Comets)	Green Onions (Booker T & The MGs	Sweet Caroline (Status Quo)

This list barely scratches the surface, however, so I would advise students to listen for and try to identify as many examples of the blues progression as they can.

Now, if you're anything like I was at the start of my musical journey, you may find this slightly confusing - surely every song should be different and have it's own chord progression, right?

Well... no. There are only twelve notes in the entirety of music. This means there really are only a finite number of ways of combining those notes, and only a finite number of those will actually sound good. So it's almost inevitable that you'll see the same chord progressions cropping up time and time again. Understanding the pattern of the 12 bar blues means you'll be able to predict (to a large extent, at least) where the song is likely to go and therefore how to play it.

Most forms of modern rock and pop music owe at least an indirect debt to the blues - for example, thrash metal evolved from classic metal bands like Iron Maiden and Guns 'n' Roses, who in turn took influence from bands such as AC/DC, Led Zeppelin and Deep Purple.. who, in *their* turn were heavily influenced by Hendrix, Cream, The Rolling Stones - and every one of those bands was inspired by the electric blues of players like B.B., Freddie, and Albert King, who represented an evolution of the basic Delta blues such as W.C Handy and Robert Johnson.

Suffice it to say... without the blues, music as we know it today simply would not exist.

2D) THE 12 BAR BLUES CONT.

I've written the 12 bar blues progression out in three different keys - don't worry about what that means right now, as the explanation is unlikely to make much sense yet! We'll do a Jargon Buster on that a little later - promise.

You can mix up any of the *whole note/ semibreve*, *minim/ half note* or *crotchet/quarter note* rhythms, but I've demonstrated them on the accompanying audio with crotchet rhythms.

Pay close attention to counting the correct number of bars. This symbol: ⁒ tells you to repeat the previous bar.

Although there are many different variations on the blues chord progression, I've kept things basic and simple here.

12 Bar Blues (A) | AUDIO - TRACK 33   BACKING - TRACK 34 |

// A / ⁒ / ⁒ / ⁒ / D / ⁒ /

/ A / ⁒ / E / D / A / E //

12 Bar Blues (G) | AUDIO - TRACK 35   BACKING - TRACK 36 |

// G / ⁒ / ⁒ / ⁒ / C / ⁒ /

/ G / ⁒ / D / C / G / D //

12 Bar Blues (D) | AUDIO - TRACK 37   BACKING - TRACK 38 |

// D / ⁒ / ⁒ / ⁒ / G / ⁒ /

/ D / ⁒ / A / G / D / A //

STAGE 2 PRACTICE ROUTINE

15 - 30 minutes per day:

1) Warm up (3 - 5 minutes): Spider exercise with position shift variation

2) New material (10-20 minutes): Chords and songs.

While your concentration is engaged and your mind is fresh, this is the time to be trying out and absorbing new concepts.

Practice the individual chords and changes as arpeggios first, then strum through them in order, and then attempt the song as written.

As your repertoire develops, you can use the more familiar songs as warm up exercises in themselves to help you develop your chord changing skills.

Don't expect instant results - as with all skills, there is a learning curve involved! But persevere, and pay attention to the results, and you will get there - most likely quicker than you think.

3) Warm down (2-5 minutes) : Riffs and improvisation.

It's always important to end a practice session feeling good about yourself, so finish off with something you know you can make sound good!

It's also important to develop your own voice on the instrument - your guitar is not simply there to play music someone else has written and "pre-approved"! At a very basic level, mess around with the chords you've learned - try putting them in different orders, try tweaking the shapes... add/ remove a finger, slide the shape around the fretboard, see what catches your ear - all the good songs have not yet been written, so get stuck in.

STAGE 3: BASIC TRAINING

GOALS:

In this section of the book you will learn

– new rhythms

– basic chord theory

– how to extend your chord vocabulary with minor and suspended chords

– how to use dynamics to improve the overall sound of your playing

3A) NEW RHYTHMS: QUAVERS

So far we've dealt with the *semibreve/ whole note* (one note every four beats), represented by this symbol: 𝅝

The *minim/ half note* (one note every two beats), represented by this symbol: 𝅗𝅥

And the *crotchet/ quarter note* (one note per beat), represented by this symbol: 𝅘𝅥

Our next step is going to be the *quaver* or *eighth note*, meaning a note worth half a beat.

The quaver is represented by this symbol: 𝅘𝅥𝅮 denoting a single quaver, and by this one: 𝅘𝅥𝅮𝅘𝅥𝅮 representing two quavers (occupying the same amount of space as one crotchet).

In addition, quaver strumming patterns are often notated with this symbol: ⌐ representing a single quaver strum, or this one: ⊓ representing two quaver strums played together. Finally, we have the quaver rest, represented by this symbol: 𝄾 signifying a half beat pause.

Try this with each of the Big 5 chord shapes in turn:

⊓ ⊓ ⊓ ⊓ ↓↑ ↓↑ ↓↑ ↓↑	AUDIO - TRACK 39

Count: 1 & 2 & 3 & 4 &
Strum: down-up, down-up, down-up, down-up

Make sure you keep your wrist relaxed, and ensure that on the downbeats (the 1, 2, 3, 4) you're strumming down (towards the floor) and on the off beats (the "ands") you're strumming up towards the ceiling. Tap your foot as you strum and try and ensure your hand follows the motion of your foot.

3A) NEW RHYTHMS: QUAVERS

Now, let's try this with some songs:

Aching Breaking Heart   `AUDIO - TRACK 40   BACKING - TRACK 41`

// A / % / % / E / % / % / % / A //

The challenge here is to not get lost in the arrangement - listen to the drums to count the beats and bars, and listen out for cues like drum fills to indicate an upcoming chord change. The bass will be playing a root note, so ensure that your chord matches the note the bass is playing. Happily though, there are only two chords, so if you're playing the wrong one it won't take too much brainpower to figure out the right one!

A good trick here is to "group" the arrangements into two parts - three bars of and a bar of E, and a mirror image second half, three bars of E and a bar of A.

Chasing Automobiles   `AUDIO - TRACK 42   BACKING - TRACK 43`

// A / % / E / % / D / % / A / % //

Here the tricky part is the fact that the song's chord progression starts and ends with the same chord. This is a very popular songwriting trick - it cements the key chord into the listener's mind, providing a strong sense of resolution.

However, at the same time, it tends to confuse rookies! Try to focus on the overall *sound* of the track rather than religiously counting beats and you will find the whole thing makes much more sense. As with the previous track, try to listen for musical cues from the other instruments and ensure the chords you're playing match up with them.

3A) NEW RHYTHMS: QUAVERS

REGGAE AND THE OFF BEAT

The "off" or "up" beat is a very important and useful concept to master. The principle is very simple - playing quavers, we divide the beat into two halves. The easiest and most natural way of marking the beat is to tap the foot - this is a pretty instinctive reaction to hearing a rhythm, so we can use it to help guide the strumming hand.

The foot goes down on the "down" part of the beat (counted as 1, 2, 3, 4) and up on the "up" part if the beat (counted as "and").

Count:	"one"	"and"	"two"	"and"	"three"	"and"	"four"	"and"
Foot moves:	down	up	down	up	down	up	down	up

Playing reggae is all about playing on the "off" beat and avoiding the down beat, creating a fun "bouncing" kind of rhythm. This rhythm is also used in plenty of songs that wouldn't be considered reggae - "Sex On Fire" by the Kings Of Leon, and "Symphony Of Destruction" by Megadeth are examples that spring to mind. Mastering the offbeat is going to come in very handy as our rhythm playing gets more sophisticated.

Let's try this simple strumming exercise as a primer:　　AUDIO - TRACK 44

Count:	"one - and - two - and - three - and - four - and" , "one - and - two - and - three - and - four - and"
Strum:	down - up - down - up - down - up - down - up　,　down - up - down - up - down - up - down - up

It's very important to keep the strumming hand moving for every eighth note, just strumming the air for the down beats. This keeps a constant movement - much like the pendulum on a clock - and allows your strumming hand to learn to "feel" the rhythm instinctively. Players who master this art always have a pleasing sense of fluidity and motion to their rhythm, whereas those who ignore it sound stiff and amateurish.

Now , let's try this with a song, in the style of the late great Bob Marley:

Three Massive Birds:　　AUDIO - TRACK 45　　BACKING - TRACK 46

// A / E / A / D / A / E / D / A //

3A) NEW RHYTHMS: QUAVERS

SYNCOPATED RHYTHMS

In this section, we're going to start making things more interesting by mixing up all the rhythmic elements we've covered so far - crotchets, quavers, upbeats and downbeats - to create more advanced *syncopated* rhythms to liven up your playing.

JARGON BUSTER - *SYNCOPATION*

Syncopation is essentially the art of making rhythm *interesting*.

A simple crotchet rhythm can be appropriate and exciting especially when played with enough energy and dynamism, but we can also generate interest by playing where the listener is not expecting (usually off beats) and leaving space where the listener would expect to hear sound.

One of the all time classic examples of a highly syncopated groove underpinning a song is "Sympathy For The Devil" by the Rolling Stones, but there are thousands that rely on a distinctive rhythm to propel them - "Hush" by Deep Purple, "Higher & Higher" by Jackie Wilson and "Are You Gonna Be My Girl" by Jet are just a few examples that come immediately to mind.

Learn to listen to and absorb the commonly heard syncopations - you'll be surprised how many crop up time and time again!

Let's try this with some songs:

Tame Thing:

AUDIO - TRACK 47   BACKING - TRACK 48

Rhythm:	♩		♩		♪	♪	♩	
Count:	1	&	2	&	3	&	4	&
Strum:	Down	**Up**	Down	Up	Down	**Up**	Down	Up

*(NB - only strum the strings those strokes written in **bold** type - for the others, keep the hand moving but strum the air! See previous page for an explanation of this technique)*

Chords: // A   D / E   D //

PRACTICE TIP:

Separate out the elements of this song before you attempt the whole thing - for example, first ensure that you can change cleanly between the chords, and then map out the structure of the song just using a simple crotchet rhythm.

Then, try counting out and clapping the rhythm, getting a feel for the sound you're trying to create.

Once you can clap the rhythm, then try strumming it on each chord, then try putting the entire song together. Trying to do everything at once is a sure recipe for frustration!

SYNCOPATED RHYTHMS: STUDY PIECE

Now, here's a study piece based on the style of one of the all-time great rock bands, the mighty AC/DC! This piece features a great deal of space, so make sure that you keep your foot tapping out the downbeats (the 1,2,3,4) and keep your strumming hand moving in time with it. For the beats when you're not playing, just strum the air - keep everything moving.

Motorway To Heaven

AUDIO - TRACK 49   BACKING - TRACK 50

Verse:

A	A		D	D		G	G		D	D		G		D	
1	&	2	&	3	&	4	&	1	&	2	&	3	&	4	&
Down	**Up**	Down	Up	**Down**	Up	**Down**	Up	Down	**Up**	Down	Up	**Down**	Up	**Down**	Up

A	A		D	D		G	G							G	D
1	&	2	&	3	&	4	&	1	&	2	&	3	&	4	&
Down	**Up**	Down	Up	**Down**	Up	**Down**	Up	Down	**Up**	Down	Up	Down	**Up**	**Down**	Up

Chorus:

A		A		A	A	G	G	A	A		D	D		G	
1	&	2	&	3	&	4	&	1	&	2	&	3	&	4	&
Down	**Up**	Down	Up	**Down**	Up	**Down**	Up	Down	**Up**	Down	Up	**Down**	Up	**Down**	Up

Song Structure: Verse x2 - Chorus - Verse - Chorus - Verse (with guitar solo) - Chorus x2

Listen to the audio and trace the song's progress to start with, familiarise yourself with the arrangement, and then get stuck in!

3B) NEW CHORDS: MINOR CHORDS

In this section, we're going to expand your chord vocabulary by looking at the sad and sorrowful world of the minor chord.

So, what is a minor chord, and why is it useful?

Well, as we discussed earlier, a chord is simply a group of notes that, when played together, make a particular mood or emotion. So far, all the chords we've looked at have been *major*, happy sounding - which is all well and good for when you want to sing songs about how beautiful the world is and how much you love ice cream and laughing with your girlfriend while wearing gumdrop smiles as your puppy dog plays by a river of chocolate.

But what about when you want to express the darker side of life, when you're sad because your girlfriend broke up with you, or your puppy died, or you've stubbed your toe? Well, this is where you're going to need the mournful, melancholic *minor* chord.

CHORD THEORY - JUST THE FACTS

Major and minor chords each have three parts (known as *intervals*) to them - the *root note*, the *third*, and the *fifth*. Each of these parts performs a different function:

The root, just like you would expect from it's name, is the start point for the chord. Just like a tree grows from its roots, a chord "grows" from its root note.

The fifth thickens and fills out the sound without really adding anything to the mood of the chord. It's kind of like filling out a sandwich with some innocuous cheese spread - doesn't really add to the flavour, but pads the whole thing out a bit, and helps the chord sound full.

The third is the interesting one, as this note sets the mood of the chord. A major third gives a happy, melodic sound (major chord), but if we flatten the third (i.e. force it down one semitone, or one fret) we create a minor third (sometimes called a flat third) and with it the sad, funereal sound of a minor chord.

But wait, you say - all the chord shapes we've learnt so far have more than three notes, how can this be?

To which I answer - patience, youngling. Revealed all will be.

In fact, as with all things musical, the answer is very simple - these chord shapes include the same notes two or more times to create a fuller, bigger sound, as this diagram below shows:

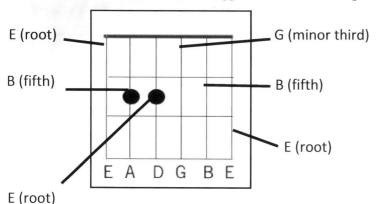

E (root) ⎯⎯ G (minor third)

B (fifth) ⎯⎯ B (fifth)

E (root)

E A D G B E

E (root)

The big six string E minor shape contains three E notes, two B's and a G - only three *different* pitches.

Keep note of whereabouts in the shapes (or *voicings*, if we're getting technical)- this will help you to make sense of some of the more advanced shapes coming next.

3B) NEW CHORDS: MINOR CHORDS

These first two chord shapes are included more in the interests of completeness than anything else, as they're real finger twisters. Have a go by all means, but don't go beating yourself up if you can't manage them! The main focus will be on the Am, Dm and Em chords

THE C MINOR CHORD (TRACK)

Here is our original C shape: .....and then we flatten the third, resulting in C minor (Cm for short):

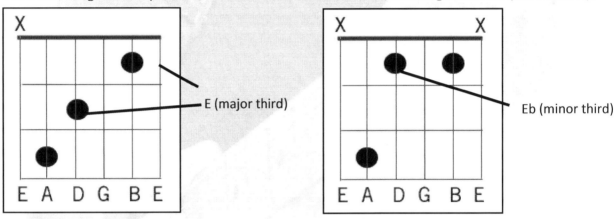

By now these chord grid illustrations should be familiar, but if you're unsure, go back to **Chapter 2B - The Big Five Chords** for an explanation

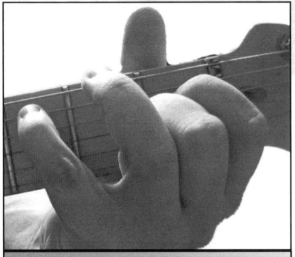

Note the fingering - little finger, third fret, A string, first finger, first fret D string and second finger first fret B string.

Only one note has moved, but a lot of fingers have had to move to accommodate it!

(left) the Cm chord, *(below)* the Cm chord written in both standard notation and tablature

3B) NEW CHORDS: MINOR CHORDS

THE G MINOR CHORD (TRACK 52)

Here is our original G shape: …..and then we flatten the third, resulting in G minor (Gm for short):

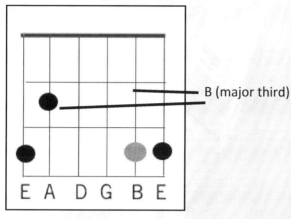

B (major third)

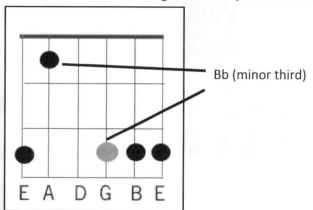

Bb (minor third)

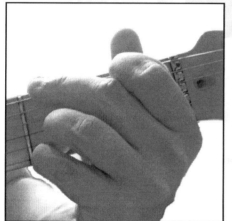

(left) the Gm chord, *(below)* the Gm chord written in both standard notation and tablature

Gtr I

THE D MINOR CHORD (TRACK 53)

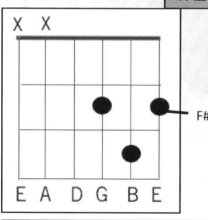

F# (major third)

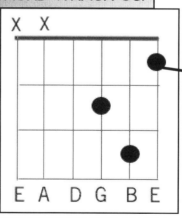

F (minor third)

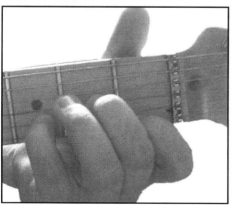

(left) the Dm chord, *(right)* the Dm chord written in both standard notation and tablature.

NB. - I use my little finger for the note on the B string, you may prefer to use your third.

Gtr I

3B) NEW CHORDS: MINOR CHORDS

THE A MINOR CHORD (TRACK 54)

Here is our original A shape: .....and then we flatten the third, resulting in A minor (Am for short):

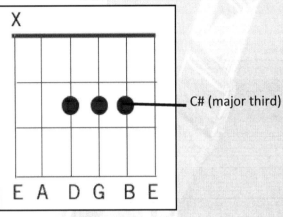

C# (major third)

C (minor third)

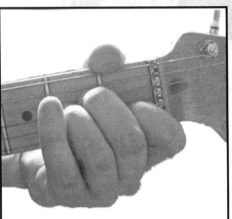

(left) the Am chord, *(below)* the Am chord written in both standard notation and tablature

THE E MINOR CHORD (TRACK 55)

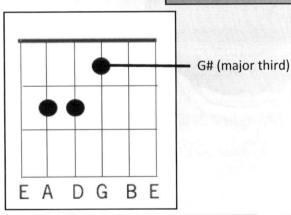

G# (major third)

G (minor third)

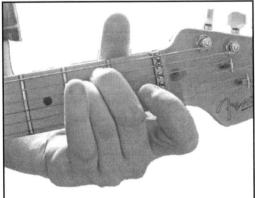

(left) the Em chord, *(right)* the Em chord written in both standard notation and tablature.

3B) NEW CHORDS: MINOR CHORDS

Time to put these new chords to use and play some songs - we'll begin with our old friend, the 12-bar blues:

12 Bar Blues (Am)   AUDIO - TRACK 56   BACKING - TRACK 57

Rhythm:

// Am / ⁒ / ⁒ / ⁒ / Dm / ⁒ /

/ Am / ⁒ / Em / Dm / Am / Em //

Stand Next To Me   AUDIO - TRACK 58   BACKING - TRACK 59

1	&	2	&	3	&	4	&
Down	**Up**	Down	Up	Down	Up	**Down**	Up

// G / ⁒ / Em / ⁒ / C / D / G / //

Never Stop Believin'   AUDIO - TRACK 60   BACKING - TRACK 61

1	&	2	&	3	&	4	&
Down	**Up**	Down	Up	Down	Up	**Down**	Up

// G / D / Em / C //

3B) NEW CHORDS: SUSPENDED CHORDS

Suspended chords (or *sus* chords for short) are a great sounding, easy to play additionto your chord vocabulary and can help to add a sense of motion and movement to your rhythm playing. There are two variants of suspended chord, the suspended 4th (sus4) and suspended 2nd (sus2).

Sus chords are so named because they are neither major nor minor, producing neither a happy nor sad sound, but instead a spacey, dreamy, unresolved feel. This is because the third - as we saw, the third is the part of the chord that gives it a major quality, and flattening the third makes it minor - is simply removed and replaced with a different note.

In the case of a sus4, the third is replaced with a fourth (found on the fretboard one fret higher than a major third), meaning the chord is built from the root, fourth and fifth intervals. In the case of a sus2, the third is replaced with - you guessed it - a second (found on the fretboard two frets lower than the major third, meaning the chord is built from the root, second and fifth intervals.

Don't worry. It's much simpler than it sounds. Let's take our Big 5 chord shapes and alter them into sus4 and sus 2 versions.

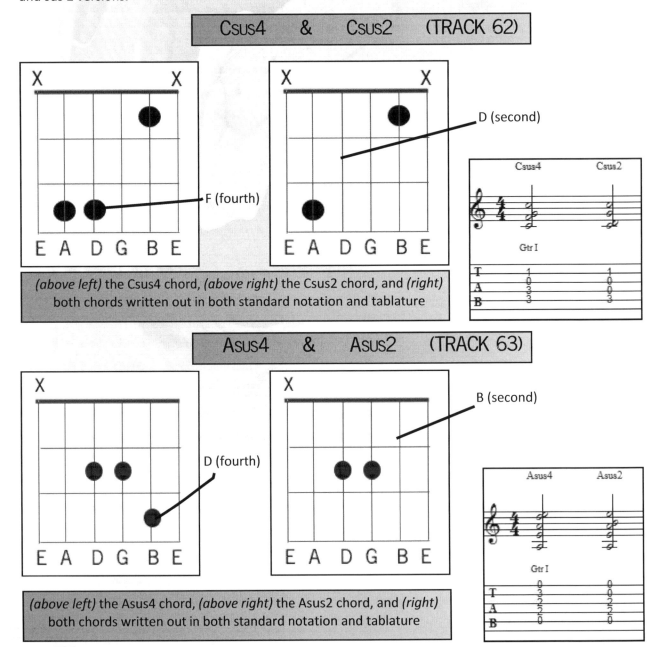

Csus4 & Csus2 (TRACK 62)

(above left) the Csus4 chord, *(above right)* the Csus2 chord, and *(right)* both chords written out in both standard notation and tablature

Asus4 & Asus2 (TRACK 63)

(above left) the Asus4 chord, *(above right)* the Asus2 chord, and *(right)* both chords written out in both standard notation and tablature

3B) NEW CHORDS: SUSPENDED CHORDS

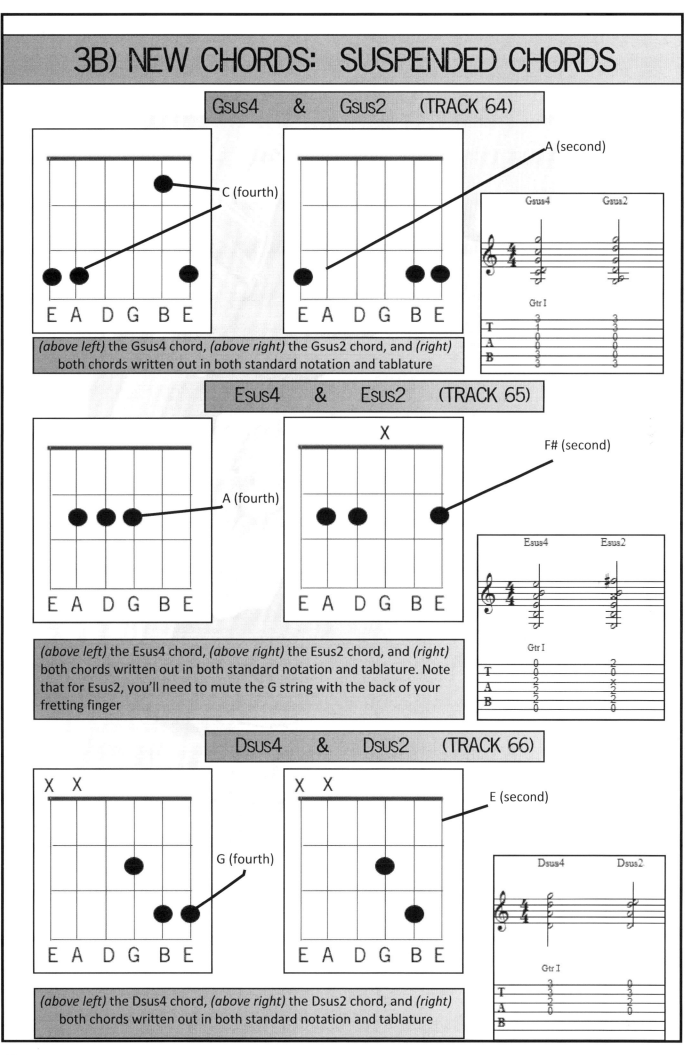

Gsus4   &   Gsus2   (TRACK 64)

C (fourth)

A (second)

E A D G B E

E A D G B E

(above left) the Gsus4 chord, *(above right)* the Gsus2 chord, and *(right)* both chords written out in both standard notation and tablature

Esus4   &   Esus2   (TRACK 65)

A (fourth)

X

F# (second)

E A D G B E

E A D G B E

(above left) the Esus4 chord, *(above right)* the Esus2 chord, and *(right)* both chords written out in both standard notation and tablature. Note that for Esus2, you'll need to mute the G string with the back of your fretting finger

Dsus4   &   Dsus2   (TRACK 66)

X X

X X

E (second)

G (fourth)

E A D G B E

E A D G B E

(above left) the Dsus4 chord, *(above right)* the Dsus2 chord, and *(right)* both chords written out in both standard notation and tablature

3B) NEW CHORDS

SUSPENDED CHORDS: STUDY PIECE

Here is a study piece that pulls together all the elements we've looked at so far and introduces suspended chords, illustrating how to use them to "colour" a chord passage without changing the underlying chord.

Don't Keep Me In Suspense | AUDIO - TRACK 67   BACKING - TRACK 68

Em			Esus4			Em			Esus2			Em			
1	&	2	&	3	&	4	&	1	&	2	&	3	&	4	&
Down	**Up**	Down	Up	Down	Up	Down	Up	Down	**Up**	Down	Up	Down	Up	Down	Up

C			Csus2					Csus4						C	
1	&	2	&	3	&	4	&	1	&	2	&	3	&	4	&
Down	**Up**	Down	Up	Down	Up	Down	Up	Down	**Up**	Down	Up	Down	Up	Down	Up

G			Gsus2					Gsus4						G	
1	&	2	&	3	&	4	&	1	&	2	&	3	&	4	&
Down	**Up**	Down	Up	Down	Up	Down	Up	Down	**Up**	Down	Up	Down	Up	Down	Up

D			Dsus4			D		Dsus2	Asus2					A	Asus4
1	&	2	&	3	&	4	&	1	&	2	&	3	&	4	&
Down	**Up**	Down	Up	Down	Up	Down	Up	Down	**Up**	Down	Up	Down	Up	Down	Up

3C) DYNAMICS

In this section, we're going to add a new dimension to your playing by investigating the concept of *dynamics*. Being able to understand and apply dynamics can add "light and shade" to your playing and can make even the simplest ideas sound more musical and convincing.

JARGON BUSTER - *DYNAMICS*

Dynamics are a vital, but often overlooked, part of music. Much as we can think of notes and melodies as words and sentences we use to communicate, dynamics are the way we say those words.

The same words can have completely different meanings depending on whether they're spoken, whispered, or screamed, so in order to make your playing sound truly musical, dynamics are a crucial element to master.

Essentially, dynamics are all about the levels of intensity with which you play the notes or the chords. The power and attack with which you strike the strings can drastically alter the sound produced.

Dynamics are about more than just volume, however. They can also affect the entire feel of a piece of music - whether the transitions between the notes are smooth and slurred, or choppy and percussive. Depending on which elements of the rhythm are accentuated, the groove of the song can feel radically different.

Dynamic differences play a huge part in individual musicians interpretations of the same song or piece and learning to manipulate them will vastly improve your playing.

Ex 1 - Volume

AUDIO - TRACK 69

There are two basic dynamic indications - *p*, meaning *piano* or soft, and f, meaning *forte* or loud. On the audio example you can hear me strumming a C chord, alternating between a bar of *p* and a bar of *f*. Try this yourself, keeping a clear distinction between soft and loud. Think of this as a distinction between "inside" and "outside" voices, if it helps!

Ex 2 - Widening dynamic range

AUDIO - TRACK 70

Beyond the *f* and *p* designations, there are extensions - *pp* (pianissmo, "very soft"), *ppp* (piano pianissimo, "softest possible"), and at the other end of the scale *ff* (fortissimo, "very loud"), *fff* (forte fortissimo, "loudest possible"). On the audio example, I've gone from *ppp* to *fff* and back again.

The movement from soft to loud is known as a *crescendo,* indicated by this symbol:

While the opposite motion from loud to soft is called a *diminuendo*, shown by this:

After playing through these examples, try and apply these concepts to the songs you've already learned, mixing loud and soft to create a more varied, three-dimensional sound to your playing.

BONUS FEATURE: "SONGWRITER" CHORDS

The guitar us a fantastic instrument to explore and improvise with, and often it's very easy to take familiar chords and add simple variations to come up with something really quite special. For this set of chords, we keep the third and fourth fingers down on the third fret E & B strings and form familiar chord shapes around these fixed notes. The results really do sound great - experiment and see what you can come up with!

Although the chord names might seem quite intimidating, don't worry about them - as we cover more theory they'll make sense. In the meantime, just think of them as interesting and cool-sounding variations on the major and minor chords we've already covered.

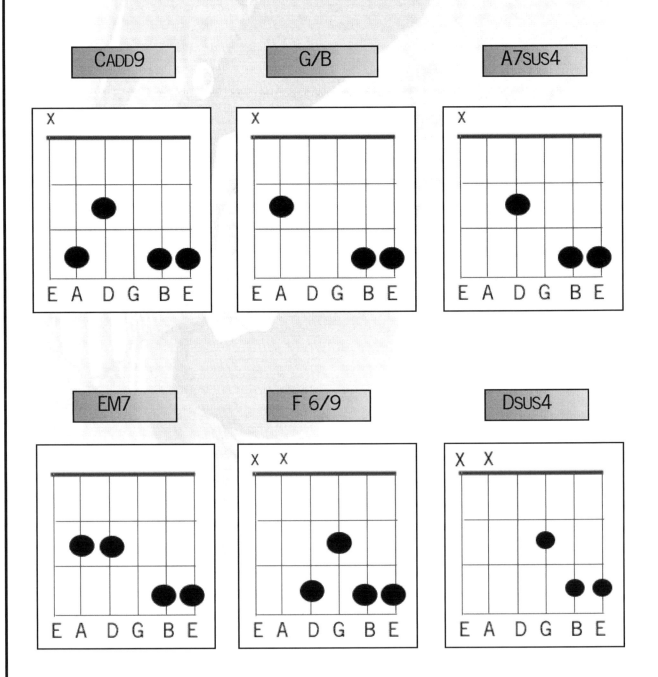

Try mixing and matching these chords with the "cowboy" version of the G chord from Chapter 1 - you'll be pleasantly surprised to realise how many expansive and "professional" sounding chord progressions you'll be able to come up with!

STAGE 3 PRACTICE ROUTINE

TECHNIQUE FOCUS - *ALTERNATE PICKING*

Alternate picking is a critical technique for any aspiring guitarist to master. Despite a slightly intimidating name, it is an extremely simple concept and with a little practice will soon become second nature.

So far, every time we've picked the string, we've used a *downstroke,* a downward motion (toward the floor).

Therefore, if you're going to play another downstroke on the same string, you're going to have to bring the pick back up above the string to pluck it again.

Why not use that motion to play a note?

Alternate picking uses the alternating down-up-down-up motion to make the most efficient use of the right hand to play the string, providing essentially twice the notes with half the effort, much as we've combined the down and up motions for strumming.

To hear alternate picking in furious action, take a listen to Dick Dale's classic *"Misirlou"*, made famous as the opening track in the movie *Pulp Fiction*. Try playing that with just downstrokes…

Below are a few exercises to help you get started.

(left) - the downstroke motion, picking down toward the floor, indicated by the symbol: ⊓

(right) - the upstroke motion, picking up away from the floor, indicated by the symbol: ⋁

Ex 1) Open strings alternate picking

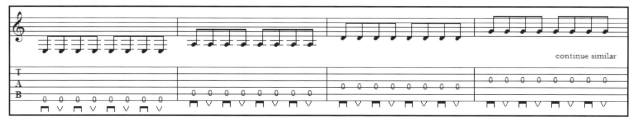

Ex 2) Chromatic double note picking

47

STAGE 3 PRACTICE ROUTINE

15 - 30 minutes per day:

1) Warm up (3 - 5 minutes): Finger independence drills. Focus on producing a clear tone, speed will come as a by product of good practice habits. Use alternate picking to play through these exercises.

Practice the above sequence using the first and second fingers, then second and third, then (and take this one slow!) third and fourth.

Practice this sequence using the first and third fingers, then the second and fourth.

2) New material (10-20 minutes): Chords and songs.

Now you're warmed up and ready to tackle new material. Take it progressively - ensure that you can move cleanly between the chords, then, map out the song with a simple crotchet rhythm before trying to add the subtleties - rhythm and dynamics etc.

You'll find yourself using many of these same changes and rhythms as you learn more songs, so make sure you train these movements into your fingers properly!

3) Warm down (2-5 minutes) : Songwriting.

Now it's time to have some fun! By now you've developed a healthy vocabulary of chords and rhythms, so try combining them to create something original and truly your own. There are thousands of free audio recording programs and apps so recording yourself has never been easier- get stuck in, get your hands dirty and go for it!

We'd love to hear your stuff, so send in your compositions to jmguitartuitionuk@yahoo.co.uk or post them to our Facebook page - www.facebook.com/JMGuitartuition

STAGE 4: MOVING ON

GOALS:

In this section of the book you will learn

– how to play every major and minor chord

– the chromatic scale

– how to come up with separate and complimentary guitar parts

- how to use the entire fretboard

4A) THE DREADED F CHORD

The F chord is a major milestone for most beginner students, as it is the first shape we've looked at in which your fingers have to form a bar across more than one string (in this case across the E and the B). Not only that, but the bar has to be formed *while* still fretting the G and D strings normally.

In all seriousness, this is a very tricky ask for inexperienced players, as it requires your fretting fingers to do two contradictory things - flattening the first finger to hold down the two thinnest strings while at the same time arching your fingers over to cleanly hold down the G and D strings. Expect a few dud notes - this one's going to take a little while.

However, as with many aspects of guitar playing, getting the thumb positioning right will help massively - experiment with your grip to find what works for you.

So why bother with this awkward chord? Well, look carefully at the chord shape- notice anything different?

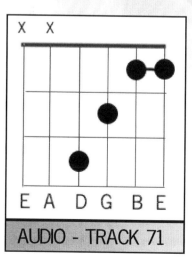

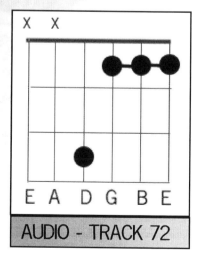

No open strings.

Aaaaaaand....? What of it?

4A) THE DREADED F CHORD

Well, this means that when we move the F shape, *every* note comes along for the ride, ensuring the integrity of the chord shape remains intact and that the sound of the chord remains the same. If you listen to what happens moving a conventional open chord shape up the fretboard, as the fretted notes move but the open notes stay the same, the sound changes radically. Sometimes good - sometimes *hideous*. With the closed F chord shape, however, we know we can get a major chord anywhere on the neck.

Most students struggle at least a little with this chord at first, so don't feel bad if it doesn't come right away. Give it time, and approach it gradually, and the finger strength and flexibility needed to perform it successfully will come.

The best way to start with this is to break it down into manageable tasks – first, begin by barring the first finger across the first fret E & B strings. Pluck each string to check that each note rings clearly.

Now, move this barre up the fretboard, one fret at a time, checking the quality of the notes as you go. You'll probably find that as the frets get closer together as you move your finger up towards the guitar's body that you need to adjust your thumb position to ensure the notes are still clear.

Next, starting from the position you found most comfortable for the barre, add the note on the G string using the second finger, and move up the neck fret by fret.

Then, finally, add the note on the D string with the third finger and do the same thing, move across the fretboard a fret at a time, checking each note as you go.

We can also alter this chord shape to a minor form – as discussed earlier, the 3rd is the element that makes a chord major, and by flattening it we can turn the chord into a minor. In this F chord shape, the 3rd is on the G string – flattening it (pushing it down one semitone) will create an F minor (see diagram on the previous page).

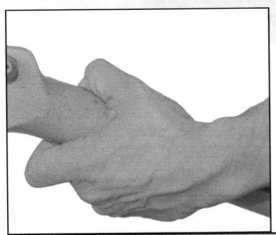 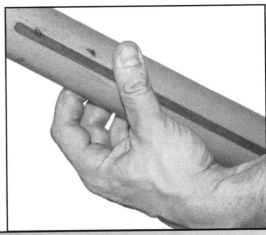

Notice the two different thumb placements demonstrated here. As the hand moves up the guitar neck, so you'll need to pay attention to adjusting the angle of your thumb to get the notes to ring cleanly. Every player is slightly different, so you'll need to spend some time on this one.

Good old trial and error - and listening carefully to the results - will get you there sooner or later though!

4A) THE DREADED F CHORD

BARRE CHORDS EXPLAINED

The F chord shape we're using here is actually based on an E chord with the bottom two notes on the E and A strings removed for ease of movement. This is what's known as a "partial barre chord", "small bar chord" or "half bar chord" depending on the source. The F minor chord works the same way - moving an Em chord up one fret and removing the two lowest notes.

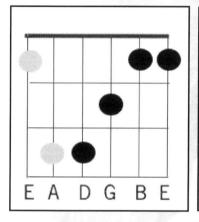

(left) the "full barre" F chord, *(right)* the "full barre" Fm chord. The notes in grey are the notes omitted from this initial partial barre version.

In both full barre chords, the first finger barres across all six strings - behind the bar the 2nd, 3rd and little fingers form the E and Em shapes you already know.

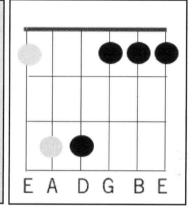

To get used to these new chords, let's try out a few chord progressions that use both open and the F/Fm chords.

12 Bar Blues (C)

AUDIO - TRACK 73   BACKING - TRACK 74

// C / ⁒ / ⁒ / ⁒ / F / ⁒ /

/ C / ⁒ / G / F / C / G //

On the audio example, I've demonstrated this with a simple quaver rhythm, but experiment with creating your own rhythms and strumming patterns to fit the backing track.

If you're feeling adventurous and want to try out some of the more awkward minor chords from Stage 3, try the minor version:

12 Bar Blues (Cm)

AUDIO - TRACK 75   BACKING - TRACK 76

// Cm / ⁒ / ⁒ / ⁒ / Fm / ⁒ /

/ Cm / ⁒ / Gm / Fm / Cm / Gm //

4A) THE DREADED F CHORD

F CHORD: STUDY PIECE

This piece mixes up both the partial barre F chord shape with some of the open chords learned so far.

What The F?

AUDIO - TRACK 77   BACKING - TRACK 78

Verse:

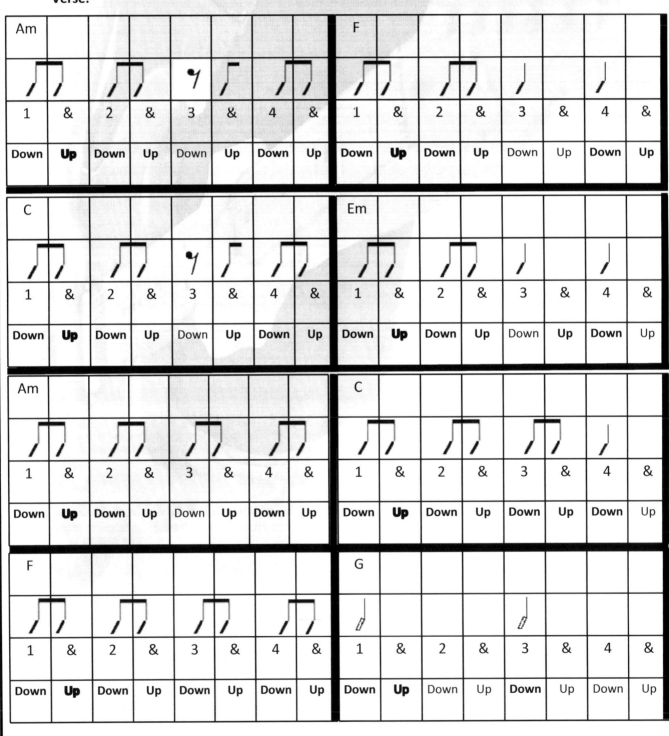

4A) THE DREADED F CHORD

F CHORD: STUDY PIECE

This piece mixes up both the partial barre F chord shape with some of the open chords learned so far.

What The F?

AUDIO - TRACK 77   BACKING - TRACK 78

Chorus:

C

1	&	2	&	3	&	4	&	1	&	2	&	3	&	4	&
Down	Up	Down	Up	Down	Up	Down	Up	Down	Up	Down	Up	Down	Up	Down	Up

G

1	&	2	&	3	&	4	&	1	&	2	&	3	&	4	&
Down	Up	Down	Up	Down	Up	Down	Up	Down	Up	Down	Up	Down	Up	Down	Up

Am

1	&	2	&	3	&	4	&	1	&	2	&	3	&	4	&
Down	Up	Down	Up	Down	Up	Down	Up	Down	Up	Down	Up	Down	Up	Down	Up

F / **Fm**

1	&	2	&	3	&	4	&	1	&	2	&	3	&	4	&
Down	Up	Down	Up	Down	Up	Down	Up	Down	Up	Down	Up	Down	Up	Down	Up

4B) THE CHROMATIC SCALE

The chromatic scale is one of the cornerstone concepts of music that it's essential to learn and understand. I am of the opinion that there are very few things in music that need to be learned committed to memory, but the chromatic scale is one of them.

So, after all the build up - what it *is* the chromatic scale?

The chromatic scale is best thought of as the musical alphabet. We can consider it the audio version of the chromatic spectrum – just as the chromatic spectrum organises the frequencies that we perceive visually as light waves into groups we call colours, the chromatic scale does the same thing for the frequencies we perceive aurally as sound waves, organising them into groups we call notes.

The chromatic scale consists of twelve notes, each one separated by a semitone - the smallest interval recognised in western music.

Take a moment to think about that. Every melody, every song that ever moved you, every symphony that left you agape, everything you've ever heard or hummed.. Twelve notes. That's it. Mind blowing, isn't it?

The standard reference point is the frequency of 440 Hertz, which we take as the note of A. At double that frequency (880Hz), there is another A note, an octave higher, and at double that frequency *another* A a further octave higher, going off until we reach pitches that only dogs can hear. The same thing happens as we go lower – there's another A at 220Hz an octave down, then at 110Hz, 55Hz etc. We divide all that frequency range between the two octaves into the twelve notes shown below:

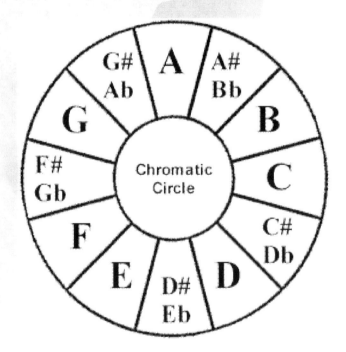

FIG 6) THE CHROMATIC SCALE

The best way to view the chromatic scale is a circle, because it really has no set beginning or end. For example, along the E string, we start with the E note produced by the open string, then the F note produced at the first fret, F# at the second fret, G at the third and so on. Notice that some notes have two names - the name used depends on the context.

4B) THE CHROMATIC SCALE

JARGON BUSTER: INTERVAL

This is the term we use to describe the distance between the pitch of one note and another. The type of interval has a huge bearing on the melody and the feeling produced.

JARGON BUSTER: TONES AND SEMITONES

The semitone is the smallest interval in Western music – it is the distance between two adjacent keys on a keyboard, or adjacent frets on a guitar or bass. A tone is twice the value of a semitone, so two frets (or keys) distance between notes.

Now, just as we can move single notes around the fretboard using the chromatic scale, we can also move chords. Moving the F chord up a semitone to the second fret will result in an F# or Gb chord, up a tone to the third fret will produce a G chord, for example. And as we discussed earlier, because the chord is "closed", no open strings involved, all the notes of the chord move together by the same amount, keeping the sound of the chord consistent.

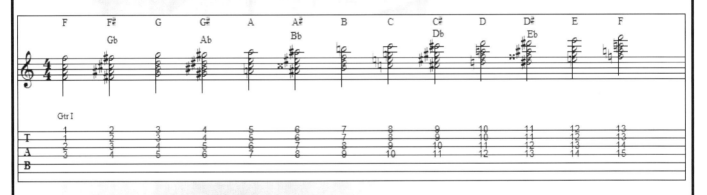

(above) The F chord shape written out in standard notation and tablature as it moves up the neck. The shape remains the same, the chord is now named after its *root note* - eg, a if started from the Ab note at the 6th fret D string, the chord is now called Ab major, or more commonly Ab.

(below) The same for the F minor shape

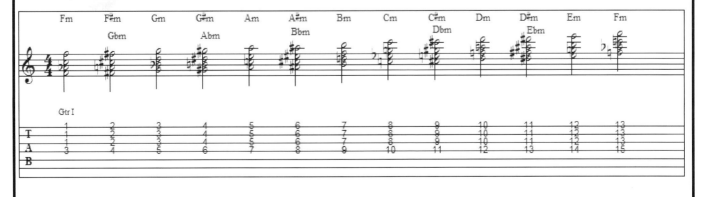

55

4B) THE CHROMATIC SCALE

F CHORD: STUDY PIECE 2

This piece mixes up both partial barre and open chords and uses the *arpeggio* technique - each note of the chord played individually - to sound the chords.

In order to get a smooth, even sound, make sure you pick the first four notes of each bar with downstrokes (towards the floor) in one clean "sweeping" motion, and the remaining four with an upstroke (away from the floor) motion.

Practice this one until you can get each note clean, it will really help to build the technique you'll need later on.

Cannon in C

AUDIO - TRACK 79 BACKING - TRACK 80

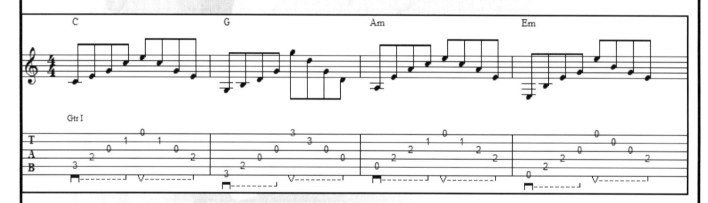

As you get more used to moving these chord shapes around, try using them to create second guitar parts for the songs you've already learned so far. This can be particularly useful if you play with another guitarist, as between the two - one playing open chords, one playing closed partial barre chords- it's possible to create a rich, varied and interesting sound.

An important note – for those new to the guitar, the F chord is *hard*. Don't feel bad if you find yourself struggling, everyone does to start with. It's simply a question of your hands getting used to the shapes and the movements you're asking them to make. Be patient, accept that it's going to take as long as it takes and keep at it.

Meanwhile, let's also take a look at the chord that underpins the whole rock guitar idea – the almighty *power chord*.

STAGE 4 PRACTICE ROUTINE

15 - 30 minutes per day:

1) Warm up (3 - 5 minutes): Diagonal coordination. This will feel very awkward and unnatural at first, but once you can see the pattern behind it and make sense of the exercise, it will start to pay dividends.

As always, focus on producing a clear tone, and begin at a very slow tempo as it is important to pay attention to the synchronisation of both left and right hands with this exercise. Be careful to ensure you alternate pick your way throughout this exercise.

Once you've discerned the pattern behind the exercise and mastered it in first position, try moving the pattern up the fretboard.

2) New material (10-20 minutes): Chords and songs.

Now you're warmed up and ready to tackle new material. Take it progressively - ensure that you can move cleanly between the chords, then, map out the song with a simple crotchet rhythm before trying to add the subtleties - rhythm and dynamics etc. In order to achieve a more interesting, three-dimensional texture to these tracks, once you've nailed down the strumming patterns, experiment with arpeggiating certain parts if the songs as used in the last study piece. This will really help focus both your fretting and pick hand technique.

3) Warm down (2-5 minutes) : Songwriting.

As before, time to have a little fun! It's important to realise that your guitar is exactly that, *your* guitar, and you can use it to play whatever you want to hear - whether it's something someone else has written or something you've heard in your head and want to bring to life. As your technique progresses you'll find it progressively easier to identify how you want to make the sounds that you imagine as you go.

We'd love to hear your stuff, so send in your compositions to jmguitartuitionuk@yahoo.co.uk or post them to our Facebook page (www.facebook.com/JMGuitarTuition).

STAGE 5: ROCK ESSENTIALS

GOALS:

In this section of the book you will learn

- what a power chord is

– how to voice power chords rooted on the E, A and D strings

– how to play a twelve bar blues in any key

– How to improvise a basic solo using the minor pentatonic scale

5A) THE MIGHTY POWER CHORD

Power chords are the basic currency of rock rhythm playing and are hugely important and useful concepts for the aspiring rock guitarist to understand.

JARGON BUSTER – POWER CHORD

A power chord is a chord which is neither major nor minor – it has eliminated the third (the note that gives a chord its happy or sad emotional quality). This gives it a driving, powerful sound perfect for rock music, as it allows the guitarist to produce a focused and compelling sound that works when distortion is applied. Major and minor chords tend to sound muddy and unclear through this sort of tone, as you can hear on the audio clip.

AUDIO CLIP - TRACK 81

We can form power chords from each of the Big Five CAGED chord shapes by avoiding or muting out the third from each shape. Power chords are also sometimes referred to as *"fifth chords"* and have the suffix "5" after them - for example, an A power chord would be indicated by the symbol A5.

C & C5   (TRACK 82

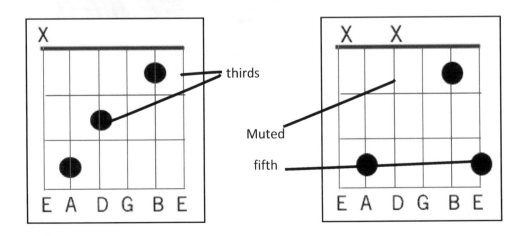

thirds

Muted

fifth

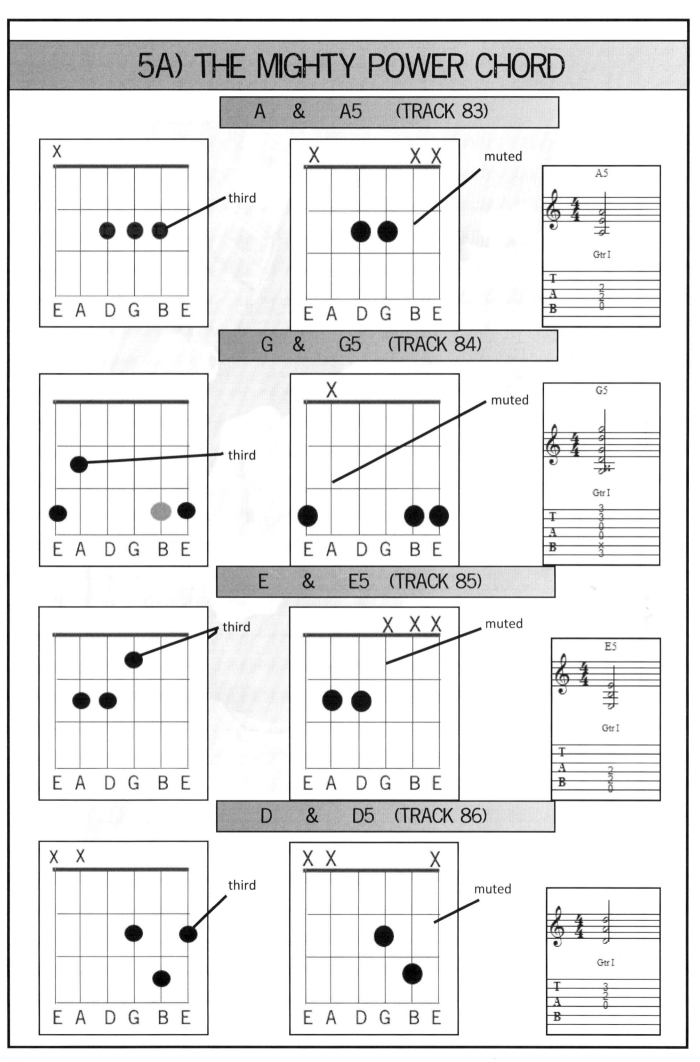

5B) ROCK & BLUES RHYTHM GUITAR

As you can see from the chord diagrams, although we can turn any of our Big Five chord shapes into power chords, the position if the third in the C and G voicings makes them very difficult and awkward to move around the fretboard. Therefore, for this next section we'll be focusing our attentions on the E, A and D shapes. We'll begin with a practice exercise using the 12 bar blues chord sequence in the key of A:

12 BAR BLUES (ROCK STYLE) : AUDIO - TRACK 87   BACKING TRACK - 88

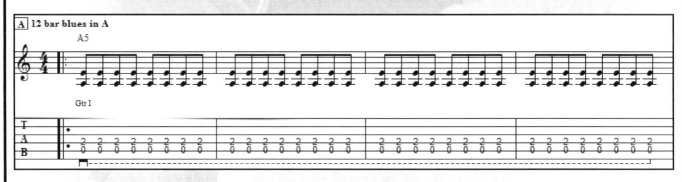

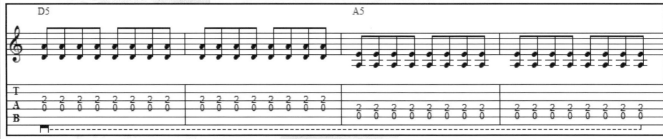

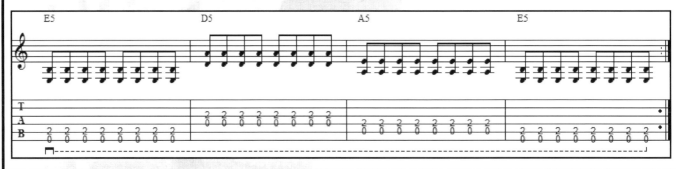

TECHNIQUE FOCUS – in order to create a punchier, tighter sound in the audio clip I'm playing the examples using all downstrokes and also using a technique known as *palm muting*.

This involves laying the flat of the hand gently across the string to ensure that the notes don't ring out too much and become messy and unclear. See the illustrations below:

(left) non-palm muted

(right) - palm muted

The more pressure you apply, the more muted and choked off the note sounds, so it's down to each player to decide for themselves how hard they want to mute the strings. Experiment and find what sounds good and feels natural for you.

5B) ROCK & BLUES RHYTHM GUITAR

MOVING POWER CHORDS AROUND THE FRETBOARD

Because they consist of only two or three notes, power chords are easily moved around the fretboard using the chromatic scale. Simply take the root note of the shape you're using (eg., if it's an E shape the root note is E) as a start point and count up from there:

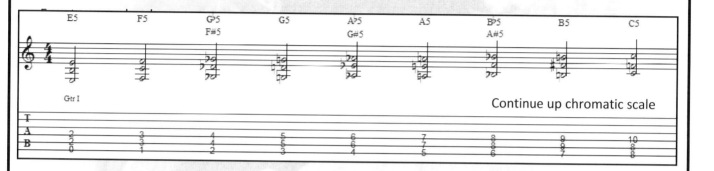

A root power chords:

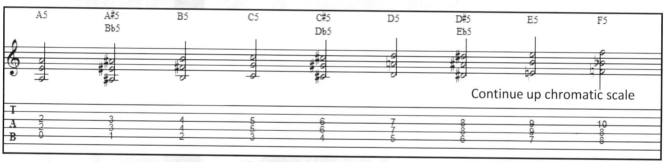

D root power chords:

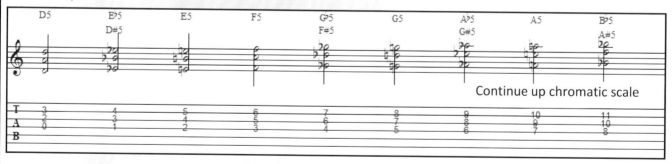

So, this gives us the ability to play every power chord in at least three positions across the fretboard. The best way to get familiar with this is to pick a note each day (eg. B) and then find three ways to play a power chord starting from that note. For example:

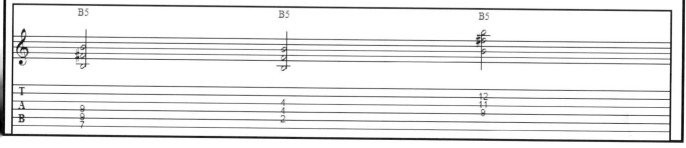

5B) ROCK & BLUES RHYTHM GUITAR

TRANSPOSING CHORD SEQUENCES

JARGON BUSTER – TRANSPOSE.

Transposing simply means moving a chord sequence so that it starts from a different note.

The trick to getting it right is remembering that *all the chords have to move by the same amount,* so if one chord in the progression shifts up three semitones (for example), *all* the other chords in the progression follow suit.

In essence, t's just like moving a chord shape up and down, except on a slightly larger scale.

THE MARTY MCFLY TEST

Hands up everyone who's seen "Back To The Future" - oh, what's that at the back? Too young?

frowns and mutters under the breath

I'll leave the main storyline to the Spielberg and Lucas estates, but the relevant part for us guitar players is towards the end when the hero, the aforementioned Marty McFly, has to invent rock & roll in order to ensure his parents fell in love and that he would therefore be born... oh, 1985, such an innocent time.

Anyway - Marty leaps onstage, grabs a rather fetching cherry red Gibson ES-355 and tells the band, "This is a blues in B, watch me for the changes and try and keep up."

Any guitar player of my generation who claims not to have been at least a *little* bit inspired by that scene is lying to themselves...

But let's pull this idea apart. What would you do if you were in that position?

A blues in B? That'll mean a 12 bar blues the way we've practiced it in A earlier on.

How to play it in B? Let's return to our friend, the chromatic scale. Counting from the A, you can see it's only two semitones (equivalent to two frets on the guitar) distance from A to B. Therefore, if we move the A power chord up by two frets, we'll get a B power chord.

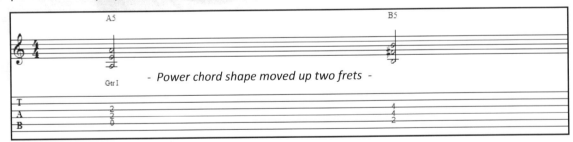

- Power chord shape moved up two frets -

Carrying on with that idea, if we move one of the chords in the progression, it follows that we must also have to move the other two chords by the same amount.

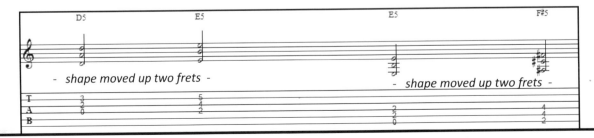

- shape moved up two frets -   - shape moved up two frets -

5B) ROCK & BLUES RHYTHM GUITAR

This gives us the chord sequence for the 12 bar blues in B that Mr. McFly was enthusing about:

12 BAR BLUES (ROCK STYLE) : AUDIO - TRACK 89   BACKING - TRACK 90

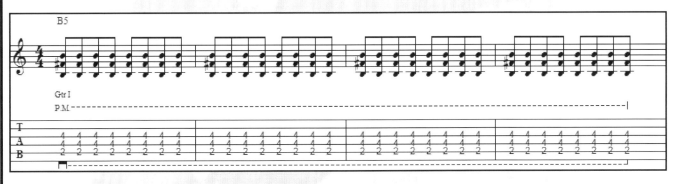

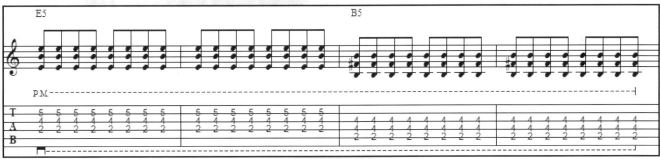

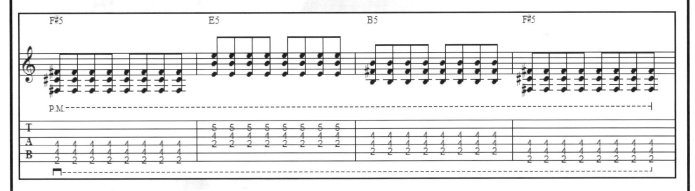

We can play this progression with a variety of different fingerings - as illustrated below:

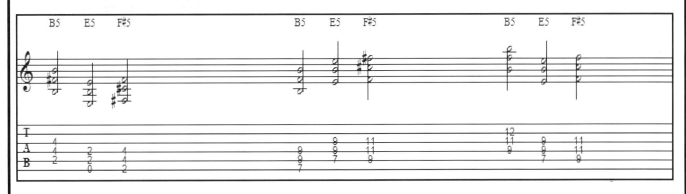

Now, to get used to this it's imperative to try it in all twelve keys – starting from all twelve notes. Just pick a different key each day and practice the progression until it's firmly embedded in your fingers.

5B) ROCK & BLUES RHYTHM GUITAR

As you get to grips with this sequence, let's try adding some more complexity to it.

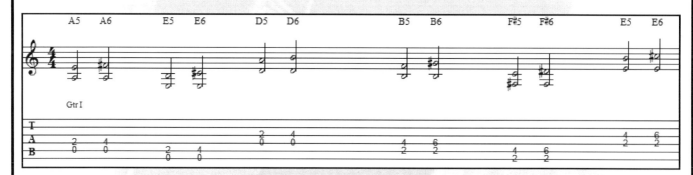

This famous rock rhythm pattern is based the standard root & 5th power chords we've been looking at, but on beats 2 & 4 of the bar we stretch out to include the 6th, a note that sits two frets higher than the 5th. This gives our chord a very "sweet" sound (don't worry about why it's called the 6th, we'll get to that in the next section), and when combined with the standard root & 5th power chord, it gives a real sense of movement and energy.

This pattern was made famous by the great Chuck Berry (although he most likely copped it from boogie piano players of the late 1940's – talent borrows, but genius steals), and innumerable blues and rock bands such as Status Quo have put it to use. I've written it out using a twelve bar blues chord sequence in C, but try it yourself in all keys.

BOOGIE RHYTHM GUITAR : AUDIO - TRACK 91   BACKING - TRACK 92

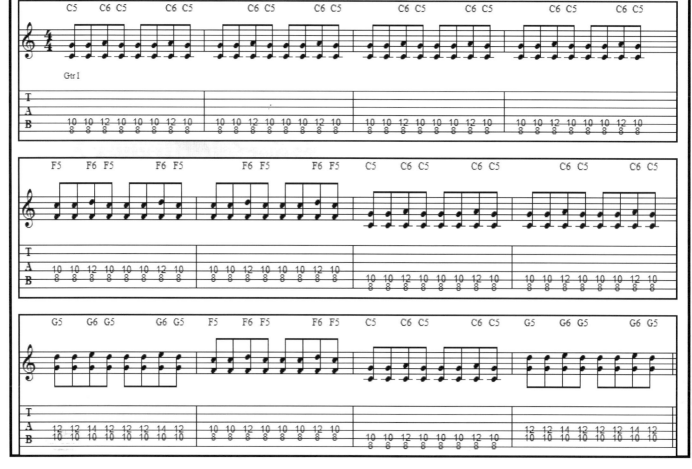

64

5B) ROCK & BLUES RHYTHM GUITAR

(left) Root & 5th power chord, (right) Root & 6th power chord variation.

If you struggle using the third finger for the 5th interval, try using the second (middle) finger.

TECHNIQUE FOCUS

As you can see from the photographs above, you're going to need to stretch out that little finger quite a way for this. The best way of maximising your reach is to move your thumb around to the underside of the neck, as illustrated.

Start further up the neck, where the frets are closer together, and gradually work downwards towards the nut. Remember, if it starts to hurt, then STOP, never force your fingers.

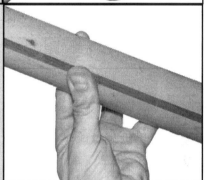

To develop this idea further, once you've got the hang of adding the 6th to your power chord playing, another popular idea is to stretch out one fret further to add the flattened seventh interval - this imparts a bluesy, mean-sounding feel to your power chords. An often-heard idea is to play the root/5th combination on beat 1, root/6th on beat 2, root/flat7th on beat 3 and root/6th on beat 4. I've transcribed and demonstrated this idea using a 12 bar blues in F.

BOOGIE RHYTHM GUITAR 2 : AUDIO - TRACK 93   BACKING - TRACK 94

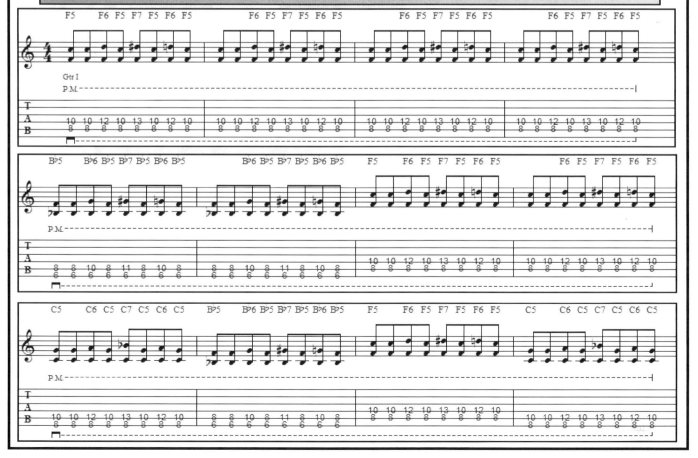

5C) LEAD PLAYING INTRODUCTION

THE MINOR PENTATONIC SCALE

Now, let's start to really work those fingers! The minor pentatonic scale is probably one of the most useful things you will ever learn as a guitarist, so let's be completely clear about exactly what this thing is.

First things first – what is a scale?

The best way of answering that is that scale is a sequence of notes separated by an interval pattern that produces a particular mood.

Next question – Why is it "minor"?

As wth minor chords, this is because it contains the b3rd interval which gives the scale a darker, sadder sound (although in this case it tends to sound more aggressive and bluesy than actually "sad").

Finally - "pentatonic"? Say *what* now?

Dead easy – *penta* is the prefix meaning five (think "pentagon" - five sided shape), and in this context tonic is not a mixer for gin but in fact means *notes*.

Pentatonic = five notes.

Specifically, those notes are the root, 3rd, 4th, 5th and b7th (again, we'll deal more with that next section, don't worry if you don't understand it right now).

And here is a handy box shape to get these notes on the fretboard:

| A MINOR PENTATONIC | AUDIO - TRACK 95 |

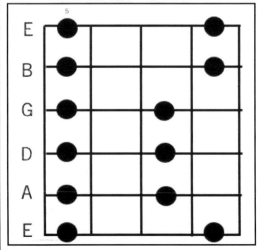

I've demonstrated the scale here in the key of A, meaning we start the scale from an A note at the 5th fret on the E string.

Obviously, if we wanted to play over a rhythm part in B, we would shift everything up two frets from A to start from B at the 7th fret, a further fret if we wanted to play in C at the 8th fret, etc.

As before, practice this scale in all different keys, up and down the fretboard to get to grips with the feel of the different registers of the neck.

5C) LEAD PLAYING INTRODUCTION

THE MINOR PENTATONIC SCALE CONT.

Here are some basic exercises to get you used to it:

Ex 1) A minor pentatonic ascending sequence in groups of three notes   **AUDIO - TRACK 96**

Notice here the use of a triplet rhythm - this is a fairly simple idea, spreading three notes evenly across a beat. Aim for a "one-and-a, two-and-a, three-and-a, four-and-a" rhythm - listen to the audio examples to get a feel for this. Try and alternate pick each note - down-up-down, up-down-up and so on.

Ex 2) A minor pentatonic descending sequence in groups of three notes   **AUDIO - TRACK 97**

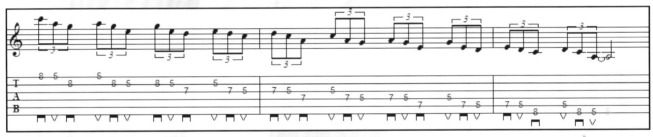

Start off with a slow tempo and ensure you can play with *complete* accuracy before starting to build speed. You're aiming to achieve a cascading feel of notes falling over each other. Players like Jimmy Page, Angus Young, Slash etc. use these ideas as the backbone of their technique. Get these ideas firmly imprinted into your mind and fingers before we move on and develop them further.

Ex 3) A minor pentatonic ascending sequence in groups of four notes   **AUDIO - TRACK 98**

Ex 4) A minor pentatonic ascending sequence in groups of four notes   **AUDIO - TRACK 99**

5C) LEAD PLAYING INTRODUCTION

IMPROVISATION: AN INTRODUCTION

Improvisation is a noble craft - the art of making things up on the spot. For our purposes, that means creating music as we go along, on the fly. For many beginner guitarists, this is a pretty intimidating prospect. How *can* you somehow magically know what the right thing is to play?

Many teaching materials will approach this by demonstrating reams of scales, licks, etc. and certainly that does have the appeal (for a teacher) of being an easily quantifiable and easily demonstrable way of educating the student.

However, it doesn't actually help you to *improvise*. It helps you to *regurgitate*. This approach serves only to train the fingers, not the mind that guides them. Improvisation begins with the *mind*.

Happily, the process of improvisation is one that we use all the time. When we speak, when we converse, we are conceptualising an idea which we then quantify and form into words. In conversation we respond to what's being said and form a response, filtering that through our knowledge of language and forming it into words and sentences.

When improvising musically, your ultimate aim should be simply to play *exactly what you want to play*, nothing more or less. In order to achieve this goal, the first thing to do is to work out exactly what it is that you want to play. You need *control*.

Now, this presents a few problems of its own. In the heat of the moment, it can be difficult to immediately compose a melody on the fly. So, the alternative?

STEAL.

Now, this isn't quite what it sounds. All of us regurgitate and reuse phrases, sentences etc. that we've heard before, whether consciously or unconsciously.

In the same way, we can recycle elements of music that we've heard and still use those elements to create something new – and one of the easiest elements to recycle is *rhythm*.

We'll begin with something simple. We'll start with one note – the A on the seventh fret, D string.

Now, think of a melody. Something you know really well – the simpler the better. On the audio I've used the tune of "Happy Birthday". Firstly, you'll hear it played on one note.

AUDIO - TRACK 100

Practice this, on one note, until you can match the rhythm perfectly. Don't cheat – you'll only be cheating yourself out of the control you need to develop. Then try a few other melodies – the more the better, it's only going to develop your ear and feel.

However, it is critical that you pay close attention to getting the rhythms *exactly* right, making sure that you can control this single note and make it do precisely what *you* want it to do, no more, no less.

5C) LEAD PLAYING INTRODUCTION

IMPROVISATION: AN INTRODUCTION (CONT.)

When you're happy with your ability to control one note, let's add in a second – the G note on the fifth fret, D string.

On the audio, I've continued with the "Happy Birthday" rhythm, this time mixing up the two notes to create different combinations – different tunes.

AUDIO - TRACK 101

In this way, by taking one aspect of a very familiar tune and using it differently, we can create something entirely new. Again, practice this with two notes and any rhythms you can think of until you're confident of your ability to control both the two notes successfully.

Now let's expand our palette of notes a little further, and incorporate the C and D notes on the fifth and seventh frets respectively of the G string. The possibilities are endless!

AUDIO - TRACK 102

Once again, practice this until you're completely happy with your ability to control the four notes.

Now, let's open things up to include the entire minor pentatonic. I've recorded a solo using the A minor pentatonic scale and the rhythm from "Happy Birthday" - have a listen and then try it yourself over the backing track. Don't worry about trying to copy the solo I recorded, just use the notes from the scale, give yourself a rhythm and go for it!

AUDIO - TRACK 103   BACKING - TRACK 104

STAGE 5 PRACTICE ROUTINE

20 - 30 minutes per day:

1) Warm up (5 minutes): The minor pentatonic sequences detailed on page 64 make an excellent warm up routine. Be sure to focus on going slowly and clearly at first whilst maintaining strict alternate picking.

By this point, you should be practicing warm up routines with a metronome to ensure the development of a solid sense of rhythm to underpin the technique you are developing. If not, now's the time to start! For those unfamiliar with what a metronome is, it's a mechanical (or more often now electronic) device that produces a beat at a constant tempo set by the user. Old style mechanical metronomes can be purchased for £50 or so, but a small electronic one available for about £12 is equally effective. Those readers with smartphones, iPads etc. have many options to download metronomes to their devices.

Begin by finding the tempo you're genuinely comfortable with - this may be as low as 30-40 beats per minute (bpm) - at this tempo you should be able to play the exercise perfectly. Then gradually increase the tempo until you find your "speed limit". Once found, gradually increase the speed by 1 or 2 bpm per week. Progress may seem slow, but you're also building core technique which will stay with you for your entire playing life.

Ensure you can play these sequences in all twelve keys and in all areas of the fretboard.

2) New material (10-15 minutes): Rhythm playing and rock vocabulary.

Pick a key each week - or day, if you feel ambitious - and work out how to play the 12 bar blues in that key using the power chords and Chuck Berry - style accompaniment patterns. It's also worth playing the associated minor pentatonic scale. It can be useful to investigate early rock 'n' roll tracks by artists like Chuck Berry, Little Richard etc as you'll see these patterns in action

3) Warm down (5-10 minutes) : Improvisation

A wonderful and incredibly simple activity to practice improvisation is an exercise I often use with my students I call "two bars on, two bars off". The idea is very simple - either using a metronome, or a drumbeat, or even just setting up and tapping a pulse with your own foot, you play two bars of accompaniment before switching to two bars of improvised lead playing, and then back to rhythm.

For example, if the key for today is C, play two bars of a C power chord before switching to C minor pentatonic for improvisation, and so forth

Continue switching between them to build a sense of phrasing and "time" to your lead playing - however, it's imperative not to cheat! Keep to the beat at all times. You're learning not just the notes but how to place them within a rhythm, which is a crucial and often overlooked skill for aspiring lead guitar players.

STAGE 6: TAKING THE LEAD

GOALS :

In this section of the book you will learn to develop your lead guitar skills using:

- string bending, vibrato and slides

— build speed using hammer-ons and pull -offs

– how to structure a solo using note targeting and motif development

— How to enhance your vocabulary using the Magic Three Notes and the Three Frets Back rule.

6A) ARTICULATION

Having acquired a basic familiarity with the tools of lead playing in the previous chapter, let's now start to really hone and enhance those skills. In this section you're going to learn how to use the minor pentatonic to create powerful and authentic sounding solos of your own.

We're going to use the good old 12 bar blues as a framework to practice on, but for this section we'll be in the key of D. This is because we're going to talk about techniques like string bending, and string bending is much easier to do higher up the fretboard.

Take a moment to work out for yourself where the power chords for the rhythm part will be played, and where you'll play the minor pentatonic before checking the tab. If you were wrong, go back and read over the section about transposing chord sequences and patterns again, as that stuff is important to understand. It's okay, I'll wait.

Rhythm part:

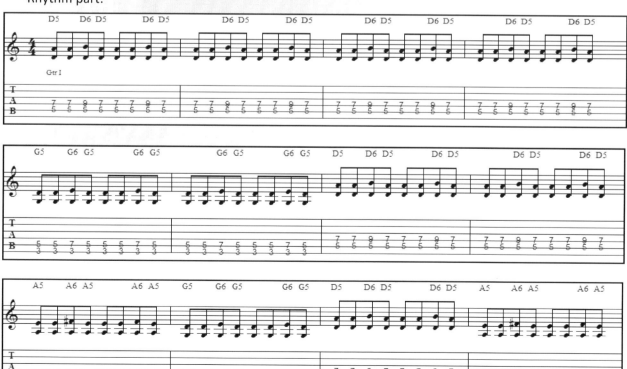

6A) ARTICULATION

D minor pentatonic:

(musical notation and tablature for D minor pentatonic scale — Gtr I)

Were you right?

Of course you were - this isn't rocket science, it's just rock 'n' roll.

All that's happened is we've moved five semitones up the chromatic scale from A to D, so EVERYTHING we were playing earlier has shifted up by five semitones as well. You'll notice that the frets are a lot closer together up here, and that's going to make some of these techniques a little easier physically.

ARTICULATION

The notes of the minor pentatonic give us a fine vocabulary for creating stinging, bluesy solos. Byt the notes themselves are really only half the story – as with speech, it's not just the words you use but how you use them that is critical to convey meaning. The guitar gives us a great many ways of articulating the same note to create different effects.

TECHNIQUE 1) STRING BENDING

String bending is the classic wailing, crying, soulful sound of the electric guitar, and it's an essential technique to master. We'll start by trying a *unison bend* – that is, two notes played on adjacent strings and the lower one bent up to match the pitch of the higher note.

The *unison bend* is a critical technique to master as it helps you to learn to tune your bends, rather than just pushing the string around randomly. The presence of the static note gives your ear and fingers something solid to aim for.

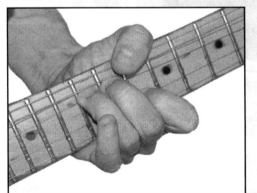

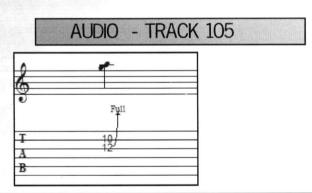

AUDIO - TRACK 105

(musical notation and tablature showing Full bend — 10/12 on B and G strings)

Using your first finger, fret the note on the 10th fret, B string, and then have your first finger fret the note on the 12th fret, G string. Reinforce it with the second finger as shown in the photo. Now, slowly push the G string note up until you hear it match the pitch of the B string note.

You may find it helpful to have your fret hand thumb come a little further over the top of the neck – this gives you a little extra leverage, helping you to "squeeze" the note out of the guitar. As always, go slowly, concentrate on pitching the bend correctly. You'll hear some vibrations as the note gradually moves up to pitch, almost as if the two notes are rubbing against each other – as these ugly sounding vibrations slow down and stop, this is your indication that the bend has reached it's target pitch.

6A) ARTICULATION

Once you can successfully perform the unison bend on the B & G strings, let's try the slightly trickier version on the E & B strings – because of the way the guitar is tuned, we'll need to perform a slightly more awkward stretch to get the notes.

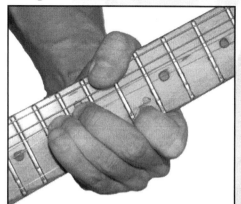

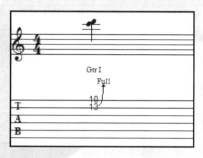

AUDIO - TRACK 106

Use your first finger to fret the note on the 10th fret, top E string, and then use either your third or fourth finger to fret the 13th fret B string. Whichever finger you use, ensure that the other fingers support and reinforce the bend.

As before, push the lower note up gradually until it matches the pitch of the E string note.

When you can perform both these bends successfully, try moving them around the fretboard.

As your ear becomes attuned and your fingers learn to gauge the amount of effort required, we can start to refine your bending technique.

WHOLE TONE BENDS

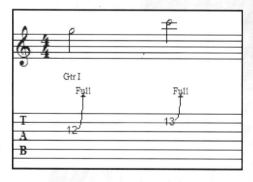

AUDIO - TRACK 107

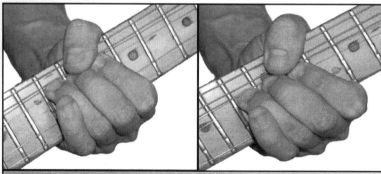

Above - demonstrating whole tone bends on the G (left) and B (right) strings.

These are just like the unison bends you've performed previously, except that here we're playing the bent note on its own without the target note as a reference. Use the audio to guide you. To help guide your ear, try playing the target note first so you have a clear idea of where you're bending to.

For example, if you're bending the 12th fret G, the note you're bending up to is two frets higher up the neck. So try playing the 14th fret G and fixing the pitch in your mind before performing the bend.

6A) ARTICULATION CONT.

SEMITONE BENDS

Semitone bends can be very subtle yet powerful tools. In essence, the idea is very simple - bending the note up by the distance of one semitone, the smallest distance possible between notes. However, they do require a lot of control – be careful here not to overbend and overshoot your target note.

In the exercise below, I first play the target note straight and then perform the semitone bend up to that note.

AUDIO - TRACK 108

MINOR THIRD BENDS

Also known as a *three fret bend*, a t*one-and-a-half bend*, a *one and a half step bend* or simply as an *overbend,* this technique involves bending the note the distance of three semitones (an interval known as a minor third). Although initially seeming intimidating, if you've mastered the first two exercises, this new bend should pose few problems as you'll be well on your way to developing the strength and control necessary to pull this quirky and cool-sounding idea off.

Players who use this distinctive idea include Hendrix, Jeff Beck and Dave Gilmour, and it adds a very powerful sound to your arsenal. As before, in the exercise below, I first play the target note straight and then perform the minor third bend up to that note.

AUDIO - TRACK 109

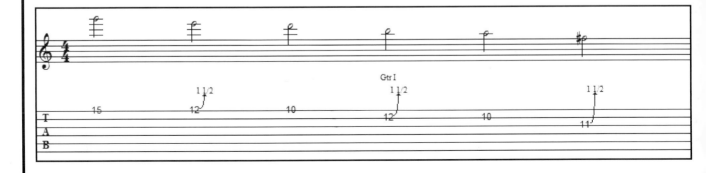

6A) ARTICULATION cont.

TECHNIQUE 2) VIBRATO

Vibrato is a related technique to string bending. As it's name suggests, the technique involves vibrating the note subtly in order to sustain it and give it a more vocal quality. Good vibrato is an essential part of any guitarist's sound – poor vibrato simply sounds like you're sustaining a note because you've forgotten what the next one should be, where as a well developed vibrato can really project a note, making it sound strong and confident.

We'll begin by applying vibrato to the notes at the 10th fret, going down the strings from highest to lowest. You'll probably find it easiest to push the string away from the floor for vibrato on the high E and B strings, but to pull down for the G, D, A and low E strings. There's no particularly special esoteric reason for this, it just means that you're less likely to pull the strings off the neck by mistake.

There are lots of different ways to perform vibrato – I've illustrated a few here:

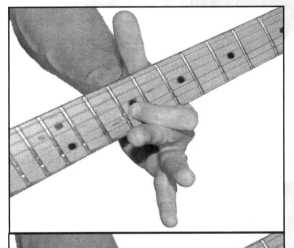

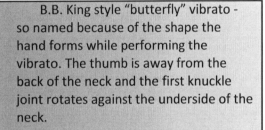

B.B. King style "butterfly" vibrato - so named because of the shape the hand forms while performing the vibrato. The thumb is away from the back of the neck and the first knuckle joint rotates against the underside of the neck.

B.B. Is famed for the eloquence and vocal quality of his vibrato. Hear it at work in tracks like "The Thrill Is Gone"

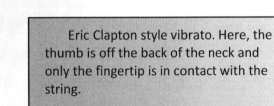

Eric Clapton style vibrato. Here, the thumb is off the back of the neck and only the fingertip is in contact with the string.

Clapton's vibrato is stinging and authoritative, you can hear it all the way from his days with John Mayall's Bluesbreakers, through the Cream years and all the way to his current recordings.

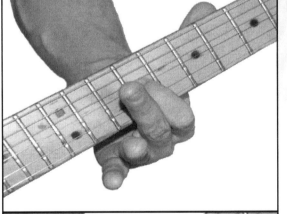

Zakk Wylde style vibrato. Zakk is one of my personal favourite rock players, with an unmistakable and absolutely brutal attack!

Here, the thumb is hooked over the top of the neck to provide leverage to get a really strident and powerful intense vibrato.

It's also worth taking a look on video sites like YouTube to see how the great players perform their vibrato – as well as the three mentioned above, take a look at Gary Moore, Yngwie Malmsteen, Albert King and Pink Floyd's legendary guitarist Dave Gilmour.

Mastering and refining vibrato is an ongoing process, but where most guitarists go wrong is by just randomly wiggling the note without really *controlling* it. We'll start by aiming to bend the note up and down by a semitone and using the following rhythms.

AUDIO - TRACK 110

Crotchet vibrato:

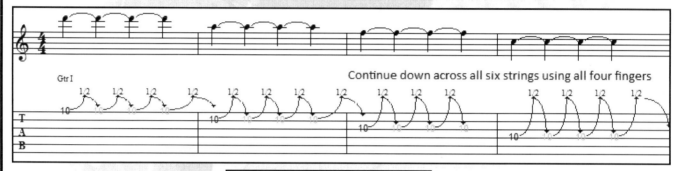

AUDIO - TRACK 111

Quaver vibrato:

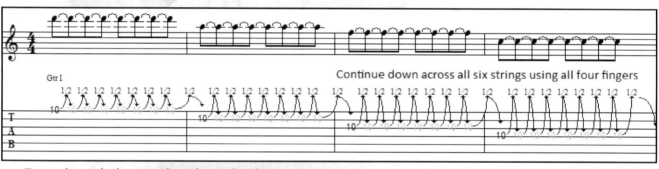

Try and match the sound on the audio clips as closely as you can, and try to ensure you're keeping to a steady pulse, whether it's playing to a metronome or just tapping your foot.

Although a subtle effect, a good vibrato technique can really bring heart and soul to a guitar solo. Essentially what we're trying to do is mimic the vocal quality of a fine singer - BB King himself described playing the blues as "singing with your fingers" - and understanding this can really help you articulate your notes.

If you listen to how a truly great singer holds a note, you'll notice that they don't begin vibrato immediately - it's held for a little while to set the original pitch firmly in the listener's mind before vibrato begins being gradually applied. Try and mimic this with your guitar playing - play the note straight, then as it starts to decay feed in the vibrato, subtly and slowly at first, but becoming faster and deeper as the note falls away. Learning to project your notes with soul and confidence is one of the most crucial skills for an aspiring guitar player to acquire.

In tablature and standard music notation,

vibrato is generally indicated by this symbol:

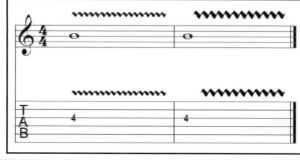

TECHNIQUE 3) SLIDING

Sliding is an often underused technique on the guitar, but it can help to add a real sense of drama to your playing. Note that this technique shouldn't be confused with playing slide guitar itself, which is an entirely different subject outside the scope of this book.

Sliding into a note is an easy and effective way of adding emphasis to a note and is quite simple to do. Simply fret the note a couple of frets below or above your target note and slide your finger up to it, keeping the pressure on as you go.

AUDIO - TRACK 112

Try and practice these sliding drills with all four fingers for maximum flexibility.

Sliding can also be an efficient and evocative way of moving between notes. Try and get your slides accurate with shorter movements before beginning lengthier slides.

AUDIO - TRACK 113

And as a way of finishing a phrase:

AUDIO - TRACK 114

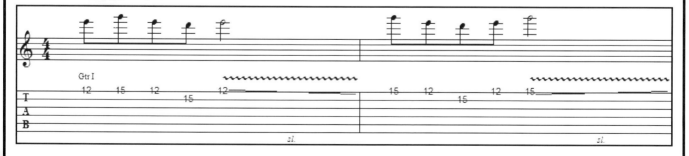

Finger sliding is a great way of moving around the neck smoothly and seamlessly - check out Steve Vai's playing for an example of a player who has made finger slides an integral and organic part of his technique.

6A) ARTICULATION CONT.

TECHNIQUE 4) HAMMER ONS & PULL OFFS

Hammer ons and pull offs are a way of obtaining a smooth, flowing sound while changing between notes as it only involves the fret hand, not the pick hand. This is also very helpful in starting to develop speed as you can generate many notes from a single pickstroke. We'll start with the hammer on, with a very simple exercise to develop strength and co-ordination.

Pick the note at the 5th fret, high E string (you should be using the first finger to fret that note). Now, as the note rings out, bring the second finger down onto the 6th fret. Bring the finger down firmly and smoothly just behind the fret (as you've practiced with the earlier "Spider" exercise). The new note should ring out clearly and confidently. Then do the same thing again, this time picking the 5th fret and hammering the third finger down onto the 7th fret, and then again hammering little finger onto the 8th fret. Once you can get the notes clear and strong, try moving the exercise down across the strings.

AUDIO - TRACK 115

Now, let's try a pull-off – a pull off is the reverse of a hammer on, moving from a higher note to a lower one with a single pickstroke. We'll try the same exercise in reverse – fret the notes at the 6th and 5th frets together, pick the string and lift off the second finger. Now, the trick to getting a nice, clear pull off is to ensure that the finger performing the pull off actually flicks the string, as that finger has momentarily become the pick. Don't simply lift the finger off the string, it needs to actively be involved in getting the pull off clear. Try and match the clarity and tone on the audio clip.

AUDIO - TRACK 116

Combining these techniques can really add a new dimension to your playing, helping you play faster and more smoothly, injecting a much more "liquid" sound to your playing.

6A) ARTICULATION CONT.

COMBINING HAMMER ONS & PULL OFFS

Let's start with that same exercise, now including hammer-on and pull-off manoeuvres:

AUDIO - TRACK 117

And now let's try reversing that:

AUDIO - TRACK 118

Now we'll try applying these legato techniques to the minor pentatonic sequences previously discussed in Stage 5C. This time, whenever we have two notes on the same string, we'll use either hammer ons or pull offs to connect the notes. First let's look at the descending triplet sequence in D minor pentatonic:

AUDIO - TRACK 119

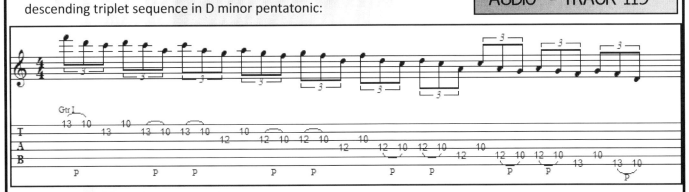

Although this sequence might look terrifying on the face of it, it is in fact based around two very simple patterns, or "cells", which we then extrapolate across the minor pentatonic.

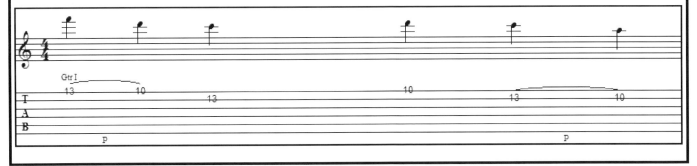

COMBINING HAMMER ONS & PULL OFFS

Let's turn that idea around and try an ascending sequence:

AUDIO - TRACK 120

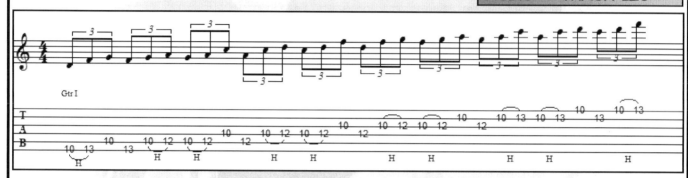

Here is the "cell" to help you decode this pattern:

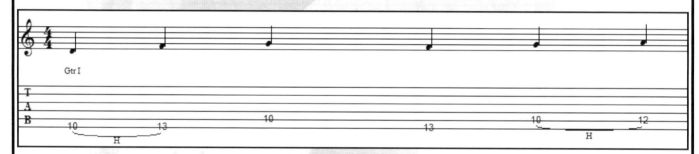

TRILLING

Trilling is a way of embellishing a note, often giving a fluttering, classical sound to a note or a melody. Essentially what you're doing is using rapid hammer ons and pull offs from a single note, giving "colour" to the note. We'll use the same exercise as we've used to practice all the legato techniques so far – try and match the audio as closely as you can.

It will take time to build the speed so try and keep the fingers and wrist relaxed, and above all be patient – DON'T try and force it.

AUDIO - TRACK 121

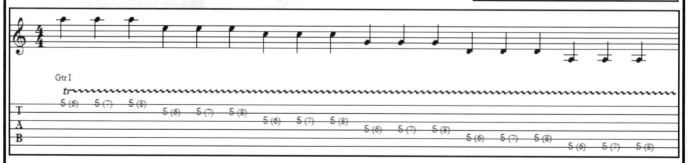

It's important to reiterate here that a smooth even sound is the important thing here, NOT simply speed for the sake of it. As discussed right at the start of the book, aim for perfection in tone and articulation before speeding up. Lumpy, ragged, uneven legato sounds terrible, no matter how fast your fingers are moving. There are a great many terrible sounding guitar players in the world. Don't be one of them.

6B) BUILDING A SOLO

THE MAGIC THREE NOTES

Most guitarists, especially when improvising, tend to rely heavily on repeated short phrases called *licks*. It is common for guitarists to develop a vocabulary of licks which we regularly deploy when improvising to help give a solo shape and melody.

A great many of the classic rock and blues licks which we often rely on are developed from a simple three note group – in the key of D minor, those notes are found at the 12th fret on the G string, 10th fret on the B string and 13th fret on the B string.

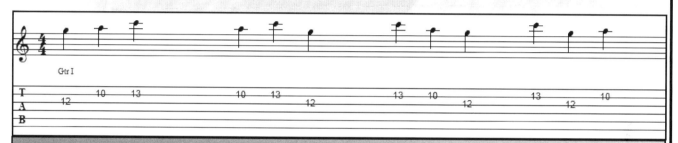

The "magic three notes" played in a variety of permutations. See if you recognise any from your heroes!

Rather than give you lots of different licks to learn and parrot out, I'd rather try and spur you to develop this simple idea in your own way. Let's consider some different ideas.

Rhythm – try playing the lick as crotchets, quavers and triplets (three notes per beat – count *one-and-a, two-and-a, three-and-a, four-and-a*). Experiment with emphasizing different notes out of the three.

AUDIO - TRACK 122 - Listen to the effect that changing the rhythm has on the lick.

Articulation – try adding in some of the sliding, bending and hammer-on, pull off techniques we looked at earlier. Again, there are some examples on the audio clip

AUDIO - TRACK 123

Now, try moving some of these ideas onto the E & B strings, remembering to account for the difference in fingering between the E & B strings and the B & G strings. I've demonstrated some on the audio.

Use these ideas as stepping stones to develop your own – remember, if it sounds good, it *is* good!

AUDIO - TRACK 124

6B) BUILDING A SOLO

SOLO STRUCTURE

There's no hard and fast rule to playing the perfect solo each time – music is a subjective field, what some people love and are inspired by, others will despise. Rather than dish out arbitrary examples, I would advise you to listen, really listen closely to your favourite solos to hear how they're constructed. Listen for:

- **Dynamics**. Is the solo just a raw burst of energy? Time to deploy some of those repeating three or four note speed patterns we tried earlier. Does it start slowly and increase in speed and intensity, or does it go for the throat right from the start?

— **Phrasing**. Many solos operate on the principles of call-and-response, tension and release.

AUDIO - TRACK 125

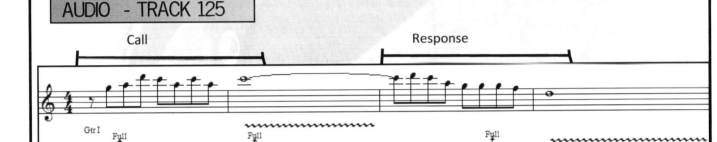

Note how in this example, the two phrases are separated by a natural pause, allowing the solo to "breathe" and giving the listener a chance to digest what they've heard. Notice also the rhythmic similarities between the two phrases, creating a motif or hook that draws the listener in.

In this next example, we have two different ways of creating tension and release – first, a rapid fire speed pattern builds momentum before letting off steam with a searing string bend. In the second, we build suspense and tension by working our way up the minor pentatonic before releasing all that energy in a fast descending speed pattern.

AUDIO - TRACK 126

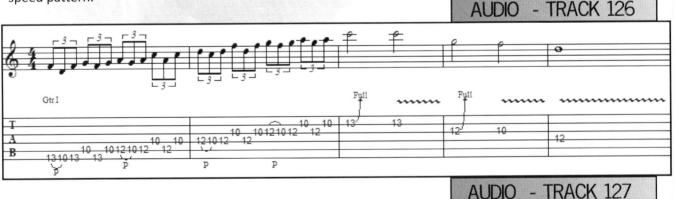

AUDIO - TRACK 127

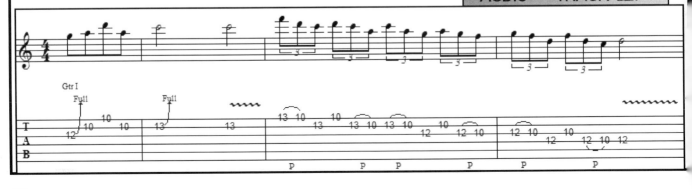

82

- **Mood.** Does the solo go from bluesy to happy, happy to bluesy (Classic examples of this are the solo in Led Zeppelin's Communication Breakdown or AC/DC's Highway To Hell)? In that case, the player is probably moving between major and minor pentatonic – more on that later.

- **Register.** Does the solo start low and sultry before moving up across the fretboard? Or does it start with a piercing high note to grab the listeners attention? Both are equally valid approaches – experiment with each.

TARGETING NOTES & MOTIF DEVELOPMENT

Welcome back to jargon central! Let's break these two concepts down. **Targeting** a note means aiming to play a specific note over a chord, rather than simply whatever falls conveniently under the fingers at the time. There is much to be said on this subject, but for the moment we'll keep things simple so you can apply these ideas directly and immediately to your playing.

Sticking with our vehicle of the 12 bar blues in D, this means we'll be soloing over these chords:

// D5 / D5 / D5 / D5 / G5 / G5 / D5 / D5 / A5 / G5 / D5 / A5 //

So, what's an obvious note to target over a D5?

Could it be....

Surely not...

A **D**?

Why yes, of course. Why on earth not? And the same goes for the other two chords in the sequence – G over a G5 chord, A over an A5 chord. These notes are known as the *root notes* of each chord (as we discussed earlier when talking about the make up of chords- go back and reread that section if you're not sure about it. It's okay, I'll wait.). In the tab below, I've highlighted where these root notes sit in the minor pentatonic box we know and love.

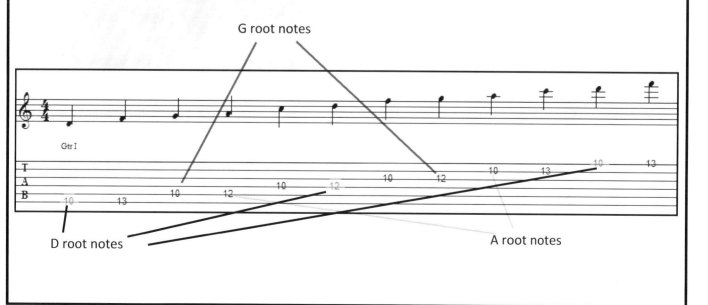

G root notes

D root notes

A root notes

Try playing just these root notes over the 12 bar as shown in the exercise below:

AUDIO - TRACK 128

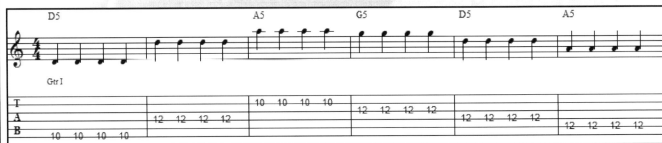

BACKING TRACK - 129

Now, let's try jazzing that up a bit.

In the following solo, I'm targeting the root notes of each chord, tying the solo very closely to the underlying chords, and also introduced a little three note motif that repeats throughout the solo, helping to pull things all together.

Before we get into the solo properly, let me explain a little about the importance of motifs and repetition.

MUSIC AND THE MIND

The human brain looks for patterns to decipher and process information, and to therefore predict what will likely happen next. Successfully anticipating it gives us a little hit of dopamine, essentially the brain's "pleasure drug". This is why white noise is so unbearable to listen to – it's completely random, and our brains just can't process that. You can try this yourself, if you have an old TV – find a dead channel, one that carries nothing but static and try watching it. Pretty soon, you'll find yourself seeing faces, circles, shapes, blobs – these things aren't really there, what you're seeing is the brain desperately trying to impose order on chaos, impose patterns on random information where there is none.

What relevance does this have to guitar playing? Well, understanding this means that you can keep the listener interested by repeating phrases in different ways throughout the solo, helping to pull everything together and create a cogent "storyline" that your listener can follow rather than simply playing a barrage of notes with nothing to connect them up. This solo provides a simple and easily accessible example of that.

6B) BUILDING A SOLO CONT.

ROCK/ BLUES SOLO IN D MINOR

AUDIO - TRACK 130

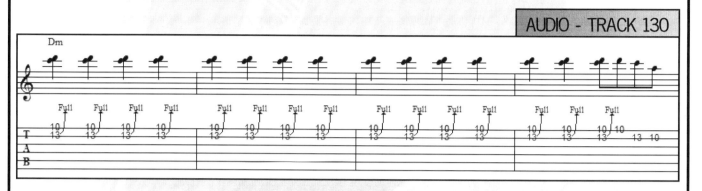

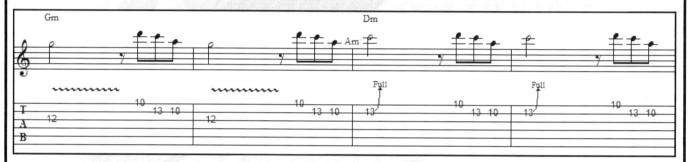

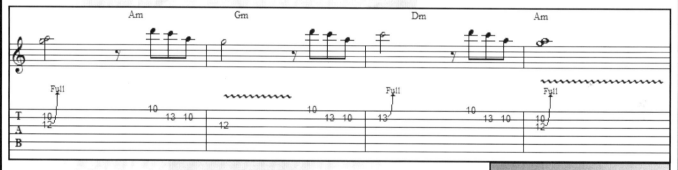

BACKING TRACK - 131

In the first four bars, I'm targeting the D root note – to make it a little more interesting, I'm playing it as unison bend (see earlier chapter). This gives a wailing, intense sound that grabs the attention.

At the end of bar four, I move down to target the G note over the G5 chord, but rather than just jump from D to G, I go down via the intervening notes of the minor pentatonic, using them as stepping stones to get from root note to root note. This creates a little three note descending figure, which I then use as a motif throughout the solo. I repeat it on the second bar of G, and then as the chord moves back to D (bar 6) I stick with the three notes, except that this time I resolve the motif back to a D (played as a string bend).

As we go into the turnaround (last four bars) the chords move A5, G5, D5, A5 and I stick with the three note motif, this time resolving it to the root note of each chord. Note that I play the A note as unison bend, and the D as a string bend to vary the texture.

When you've mastered this solo, use these ideas as a springboard for your own.

6B) BUILDING A SOLO CONT.

BONUS: THE THREE FRETS BACK RULE

This a very simple and useful way of getting new sounds out of the same minor pentatonic shape. By moving the shape three frets back, we can access the brighter, happier sound of the major pentatonic scale.

AUDIO - TRACK 132

Hang on though, that looks suspiciously like B minor pentatonic.... In fact, it looks exactly the same. So how come it's not the B minor pentatonic?

Well, here's the thing - if you play it over a B then it is. It's all about context.

When played over a B, these notes give you the mean, aggressive sound characteristic of the minor pentatonic, but when you play them over a D all these notes behave in different ways (somewhat beyond the scope of this book), giving you a whole new vocabulary – for free!

This "three frets back rule" works in any key - A minor pentatonic over C gives you C major pentatonic, F# minor pentatonic over A gives you A major pentatonic and so on. Listen to players like Angus Young, Jimmy Page and Slash for examples of this movement between scales.

Use this new scale in conjunction with D minor pentatonic over the backing tracks to add a new dimension to your blues and rock solos - experiment and find what sounds good to your ears. Below are a couple of examples to get you started:

AUDIO - TRACK 133

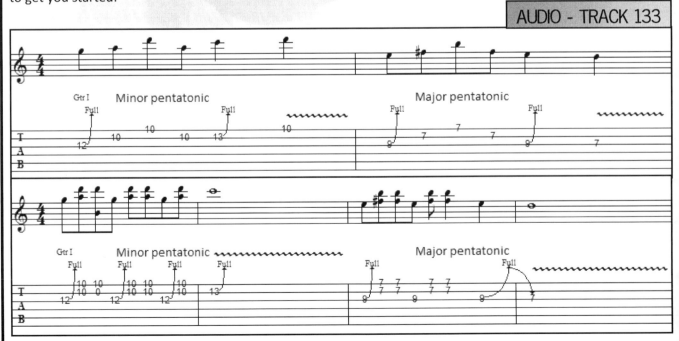

STAGE 6 PRACTICE ROUTINE

20 - 30 minutes per day:

1) Warm up (5 minutes):

AUDIO - TRACK 134

This legato exercise provides an effective way of building a strong and even hammer-on and pull-off technique as well as working every possible finger combination. Begin in 1st position (first finger/ first fret, second finger/ second fret, third finger/third fret and little finger/ fourth fret) and move up the fret board one position at a time. With my students I usually found moving through the first four positions provides a solid warm up.

Set the tempo as low as you need to to play steady even eighth notes, and then begin to progressively speed up, using increments of 1 or 2 beats per minute (bpm). Once you've mastered the exercise, tweak it - try using a triplet rhythm.

2) New material (10-15 minutes): Repertoire,   (5- 10 minutes): Technical Development

Now your vocabulary of techniques is becoming more complete, try investigating songs by early rock & roll artists like Chuck Berry, early Rolling Stones material, early Beatles and so on. There are many excellent transcription books available to help you, and these songs are the bedrock of today's music.

I'd also advise investigating punk rock bands like the Sex Pistols, The Undertones and newer bands like Green Day and Blink 182, as these bands make effective use of simple minor pentatonic and powerchord ideas, and have gone on to influence many more technical artists.

It's also worth setting aside time here to practice the sequenced hammer on/ pull off ideas and bends, vibrato etc. all over the neck to get used to the different feels of the fretboard distances, string tensions and so on.

3) Warm down (5 minutes) : Improvisation

The "two bars on, two bars off" exercise discussed in the Stage 5 Practice routine is an excellent way to warm down, but try developing the ideas in the example blues solo and coming up with your own solos over the backing track. Once you've practiced the sequences and patterns, put the track on, crank the amp and just let rip!

STAGE 7: NUTS & BOLTS: BASIC MUSIC THEORY

GOALS :

In this section of the book you will learn:

— *what the major scale is*

— *what a key is*

— *how to harmonise a scale (and what that means)*

— *The Nashville Numbering System and its uses*

— *The CAGED system and how to use this to unlock the fretboard*

7A) THE MAJOR SCALE

(NB - to make sense of the concepts discussed here, make sure you have read and understood section 4B - The Chromatic Scale)

.....and first, there was sound. Many tones, many frequencies, many pitches - and lo, it was good but it was so..... *disorganised*.

And then man came along, and divided up the spectrum of noise that we can hear into twelve distinct groups called *notes*, and those notes would be repeated through different *octaves*. And the twelve notes were arranged into the chromatic scale, the alphabet of music.

And thus was music theory born.

The concepts of notes and octaves has been discussed in earlier chapters in this book, so if you're at all unsure of these concepts go back and read over them, because otherwise this chapter will serve only to confuse...

In the beginning, there was the *chromatic* scale. All twelve notes, lined up a semitone apart from each other. Problem is, the sound is just too dense, too closely packed to really put across any sort of musical message. In order to create something melodic, we need to create some gaps in that scale – in musical terms, apply an interval pattern to it. Each scale has a different interval pattern, and this pattern is responsible for the differing sounds and moods these scales create.

For the major scale, we start by nominating a note to be the root note (the start point for the scale) and apply the following pattern:

ROOT – tone - 2nd – tone - 3rd – semitone - 4th – tone - 5th – tone - 6th – tone - 7th -semitone - ROOT

7A) THE MAJOR SCALE

Taking A as our start or root note, this gives the following sequence:

A A#/Bb *B* C *C#*/Db *D* D#/Eb *E* F *F#*/Gb G *G#*/Ab *A*

Because musical convention demands that we have one, and only one, of each letter, we would write out the A major scale like so:

A	B	C#	D	E	F#	G#	A
Root	2nd	3rd	4th	5th	6th	7th	Root

Rather than dish out unwieldy two octave box patterns, I'd like you to try playing this along the A string:

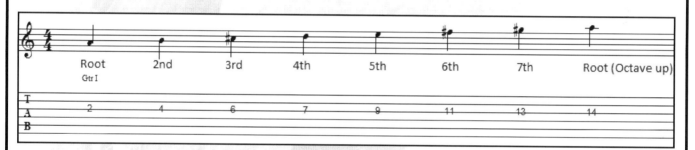

EAR TRAINING

Before we go any further, let's try a couple of simple tunes using the major scale. It's all about music, after all – the tunes on the audio all use the major scale, all start from the root note, see how closely you can copy them.

AUDIO TRACKS 135, 136, 137

WHAT IS A KEY?

Well, it opens doors, obviously. But it also has a musical meaning – if a song is in the key of A, that means that all the notes used in both the melody (ie – the tune) and the harmony (ie - the chords behind the tune) are all drawn form the A major scale, nothing from outside. This means that the notes will all work together to produce a sweet, consonant and predictable (in a good way) sound.

A song which is diatonic is strictly in one key, drawing the entirety of it's melody and harmony notes from one major scale. Non- diatonic notes and chords can be used to create tension and dissonance within a piece of music.

7B) HARMONISING THE MAJOR SCALE & THE NASHVILLE NUMBER SYSTEM

When we harmonise a scale, that means we're using the notes of that scale to build chords. Seven notes in the scale mean we can build - wait for it - seven chords. Under the Nashville Number System, we give each of those chords a Roman numeral to identify it by the position of its root note in the scale. So in the key of A, the A chord will be the I because its root note is the first note of the scale.

Trust me – like everything in music, it's much, *much* simpler than it sounds.

JARGON BUSTER – THE NASHVILLE NUMBER SYSTEM

This is an informal shorthand way of transcribing music and quickly transposing, or changing the key. Each chord is assigned a Roman numeral depending on the position of its root note within the major scale scale of its home key. So for example in the key of A (A B C# D E F# G#) the chord sequence // A / D / A / E // would be written as // I / IV / I / V //. This could then be transposed into the key of C -for example, to suit the vocal range of a different singer- (C, D, E, F, G , A, B) as // C / F / C / G //.

It's known as the Nashville Number System as it was developed by busy session players in late 1950s Nashville, where players were churning out record after record in an almost industrial fashion. Neal Matthers, Jr, vocalist with the USA's then premier backup vocal groups The Jordanaires (who backed Elvis Presley in his heyday, along with Johnny Cash, Patsy Cline, Ricky Nelson and many others). This system is hugely useful in being able to quickly identify and predict the chord changes for a song.

In the West, our sense of harmony is built on the interval of a third. A major third (four semitones) produces a happy, euphoric harmony, a minor or flattened third (three semitones) produces a mournful, melancholic quality (revisit the section on chords if you feel a little out of your depth here).

To finish the chord off, we add another note a third on top of that – the fifth.

$$Root – skip\ 2^{nd} - 3^{rd} – skip\ 4^{th} – 5^{th}.$$

Depending on what combination of thirds and fifths we get, we can produce three different types of triad chord.

JARGON BUSTER – TRIAD

A triad is a three note chord, this is the basic level of harmony that we need to produce any kind of real emotion resonance.

Root – 4 semitones - 3rd – 3 semitones – 5th This is the formula for a major chord.

Root – 3 semitones - b3rd – 4 semitones – 5th This is the formula for a minor chord.

Root – 3 semitones - b3rd – 3 semitones – b5th This is the formula for a diminished chord.

7B) HARMONISING THE MAJOR SCALE & THE NASHVILLE NUMBER SYSTEM

So now let's harmonise the A major scale.

Notes available: **A** *A#/Bb* **B** *C* **C#/Db** **D** *D#/Eb* **E** *F* **F#/Gb** *G#/Ab*

One important thing to remember - because of the conventions involving music notation, **there must be one of each letter, and only one in each key.** So in the key of A, we'll be using C#, F# and G# rather than Db, Gb and Ab.

I chord – Root: A - *4 semitones* – **3rd: C#** - *3 semitones* – **5th: E**   *Result:* **A**

ii chord - Root: B - *3 semitones* – **b3rd: D** - *4 semitones* – **5th: F#**   *Result:* **Bm**

iii chord - Root: C# - *3 semitones* – **b3rd: E** - *4 semitones* – **5th: G#**   *Result:* **C#m**

IV chord - Root: D - *4 semitones* – **3rd: F#** - *3 semitones* – **5th: A**   *Result:* **D**

V chord - Root: E - *4 semitones* – **3rd: G#** - *3 semitones* – **5th: B**   *Result:* **E**

vi chord - Root: F# - *3 semitones* – **b3rd: A** - *4 semitones* – **5th: C#**   *Result:* **F#m**

vii chord - Root: G# - *3 semitones* – **b3rd: B** - *3 semitones* – **5th: D**   *Result:* **G# diminished**

I recommend doing this exercise for all twelve keys – it should take about 40 minutes to an hour, and will leave you with a thorough understanding of the principles of harmony that you'll never forget. You'll see just how useful this becomes in practice in the next chapter.

To start with, pick a root note, then count round the chromatic scale to find the other notes of the major scale - remember the formula:

Root (tone) **2nd** (tone) **3rd** (semitone) **4th** (tone) **5th** (tone) **6th** (tone) **7th**

Chord types - ***Major*** *: Root - 3rd - 5th*   ***Minor*** *(m): Root – b3rd - 5th*

Augmented *(aug) : Root - 3rd - #5th*   ***Diminished*** *(dim) : Root - b3rd - b5th*

Scale: R   2   3   4   5   6   7
C

Number	Notes	Intervals	Chord Type	Chord
I	C			
ii				
iii				
IV				
V				
vi				
vii				

7B) HARMONISING THE MAJOR SCALE & THE NASHVILLE NUMBER SYSTEM

Scale: R   2   3   4   5   6   7
G

Number	Notes	Intervals	Chord Type	Chord
I	G			
ii				
iii				
IV				
V				
vi				
vii				

Scale: R   2   3   4   5   6   7
D

Number	Notes	Intervals	Chord Type	Chord
I	D			
ii				
iii				
IV				
V				
vi				
vii				

Scale: R 2 3 4 5 6 7
A   B   C# D E F# G#

Number	Notes	Intervals	Chord Type	Chord
I	A, C#, E	R, 3, 5	Major	A
ii	B, D, F#	R, b3, 5	Minor	Bm
iii	C#, E, G#	R, b3, 5	Minor	C#m
IV	D, F#, A	R, 3, 5	Major	D
V	E, G#, B	R, 3, 5	Major	E
vi	F#, A, C#	R, b3, 5	Minor	F#m
vii	G#, B, D	R, b3, b5	Diminished	G# dim

Scale: R 2 3 4 5 6 7
B

Number	Notes	Intervals	Chord Type	Chord
I	E			
ii				
iii				
IV				
V				
vi				
vii				

7B) HARMONISING THE MAJOR SCALE & THE NASHVILLE NUMBER SYSTEM

Scale: R   2   3   4   5   6   7
B

Number	Notes	Intervals	Chord Type	Chord
I	B			
ii				
iii				
IV				
V				
vi				
vii				

Scale: R   2   3   4   5   6   7
F#

Number	Notes	Intervals	Chord Type	Chord
I	F#			
ii	G#			
iii	A#			
IV	B			
V	C#			
vi	D#			
vii	E#			

This is where things start to get a bit confusing - we discovered earlier, there is no E#. The chromatic scale goes straight from E to F. However, we've already used the letter F, so we have to call it E# for the purposes of this key.

Scale: R   2   3   4   5   6   7
C#   D#   E#   F#   G#   A#   B#

Number	Notes	Intervals	Chord Type	Chord
I	C#			
ii	D#			
iii	E#			
IV	F#			
V	F#			
vi	G#			
vii	A#			

Oh, now this is just getting silly. Now we've had to call F "E#" and C "B#". Time to try and look at flattening the notes instead of sharpening them (we'll talk more about this when we look at a theory idea known as the cycle of *4ths* and *cycle of 5ths*)

7B) HARMONISING THE MAJOR SCALE & THE NASHVILLE NUMBER SYSTEM

Scale:	R	2	3	4	5	6	7
	F	G	A	Bb	C	D	E

Number	Notes	Intervals	Chord Type	Chord
I	F			
ii	G			
iii	A			
IV	Bb			
V	C			
vi	D			
vii	E			

Scale:	R	2	3	4	5	6	7
	Bb						

Number	Notes	Intervals	Chord Type	Chord
I	Bb			
ii				
iii				
IV				
V				
vi				
vii				

Scale:	R	2	3	4	5	6	7
	Eb						

Number	Notes	Intervals	Chord Type	Chord
I	Eb			
ii				
iii				
IV				
V				
vi				
vii				

Scale:	R	2	3	4	5	6	7
	Ab						

Number	Notes	Intervals	Chord Type	Chord
I	Ab			
ii				
iii				
IV				
V				
vi				
vii				

7B) HARMONISING THE MAJOR SCALE & THE NASHVILLE NUMBER SYSTEM

Scale: R   2   3   4   5   6   7
Db

Number	Notes	Intervals	Chord Type	Chord
I	**Db**			
ii				
iii				
IV				
V				
vi				
vii				

Scale: R   2   3   4   5   6   7
Gb

Number	Notes	Intervals	Chord Type	Chord
I	**Gb**			
ii				
iii				
IV				
V				
vi				
vii				

Notice anything?

No matter what the root note, the harmonisation process always produces the same sequence of chord types -

> **I - major**
> **ii - minor**
> **Iii - minor**
> **IV - major**
> **V - major**
> **vi - minor**
> **vii - diminished**

So? So what?

Ever noticed how some songs sound the same? Well, 90% of the time it's because they **are** the same, in terms of chord progression at least.

Examples:
Don't Stop Believing by Journey, When I Come Around by Green Day, Let It Be by The Beatles – all **I – vi – IV – V** sequences.

Twist & Shout, La Bamba – both **I – IV – V**s

Practically all blues and rock & roll songs use the same basic 12 bar structure, as do many jazz and soul songs.

Effectively, what this knowledge gives you is a shortcut to learning literally **thousands** of songs.

7B) HARMONISING THE MAJOR SCALE & THE NASHVILLE NUMBER SYSTEM

CIRCLE OF 5THS/ 4THS

Those of you paying close attention will have noticed something about that last section. We started our journey through the keys with the C major scale, which had no sharpened or flattened notes. Next was the G major scale, which had a single sharpened note (F#). G is the fifth note of C major scale.

Distance of a perfect fifth

C ⟹ G

No sharps   *F#*

Following on from the G major scale, our next stop was D, with two sharpened notes (C# and F#). Nothing coincidental about this - in fact, it was all part of my devilishly cunning plan! Notice the same thing has happened - D is the fifth note of the G major scale.

Distance of a perfect fifth   *Distance of a perfect fifth*

C ⟹ G ⟹ D

No sharps   *F#*   *F#, C#*

So as you can see, every time we move up another 5th, we gain another sharp note, moving round to the insanity of C# where now everything is sharpened!

Such a mass of sharpened notes makes reading traditional music notation (often a tricky enough task on the guitar as it is) almost impossible. So, moving in fourths and using flat notes, we can make the whole thing a great deal simpler:

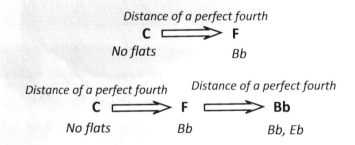

Distance of a perfect fourth

C ⟹ F

No flats   *Bb*

Distance of a perfect fourth   *Distance of a perfect fourth*

C ⟹ F ⟹ Bb

No flats   *Bb*   *Bb, Eb*

The key of Bb contains the notes **Bb, C, D, Eb, F, G, A**. By comparison, the *enharmonically equivalent* key of A# would contain the notes **A#, B#, C##, D#, E#, F##, G##**! So for anyone who's ever heard me say only a lunatic will work in the key of A#, this is the reason why...

JARGON BUSTER - ENHARMONIC EQUIVALENCE

This is simply an extremely fancy way of saying that one note can be called two things - for example, Bb and A# are the same note, C# and Db are the same note... it depends entirely on what other notes are in the same key which name we decide to give it.

7B) HARMONISING THE MAJOR SCALE & THE NASHVILLE NUMBER SYSTEM

CIRCLE OF 5THS/ 4THS

The best way to represent the sequence that results from this idea is in diagram form:

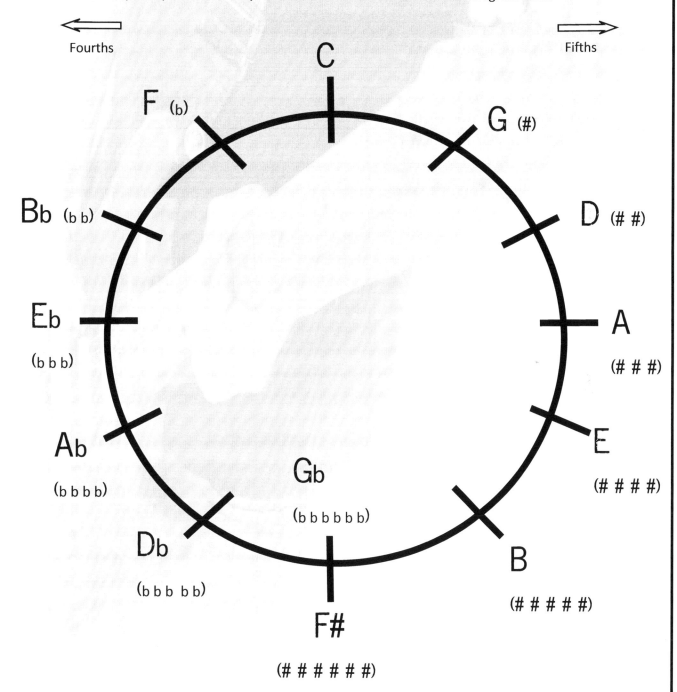

As well as a useful tool for understanding theory, this can also be used as a practice tool - I thoroughly recommend practicing licks, scales, arpeggios etc in cycles of fourths and fifths. It can also be used for songwriting - check out tracks as diverse as *Parisienne Walkways*, *I Will Survive* and *Fly Me To The Moon* for examples of a cycle of fourths chord sequence.

7C) UNLOCKING THE FRETBOARD - THE CAGED SYSTEM

The guitar is a very tactile instrument – it's all about shapes. Specifically, five of them. C, A, G, E, and D. We've already learned these basic shapes in the first pages, then modified them to produce minor versions and powerchords. Now, it's time to take the final step and use the chromatic scale to move these chord shapes across the fretboard and learn how to play rhythm and lead parts in any key, anywhere on the fretboard.

At it's heart, the CAGED system (like everything in music, just to ram the point home) is **simple.** Stupidly, beautifully, elegantly **simple**. Let's say you wanted to play a C# chord (for argument's sake).

We have five options:

1) Use the C shape and move it up one semitone (*C-- C#*)

Here we are using the first finger to bar across the first fret and using the second, third and fourth fingers to from the C shape behind the bar.

2) Use the A shape and move it up four semitones (*A --Bb --B --C --C#*)

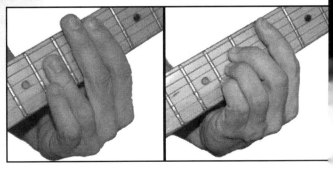

Here the first finger is barred across the fourth fret, while the second, third and fourth fingers form the shape behind the bar. As you get more experienced, you'll gradually find it gets more comfortable to use the third finger to bar across the 6th fret B, G and D strings.

3) Use the G shape and move it up six semitones (*G - G# - A - Bb - B - C - C#*)

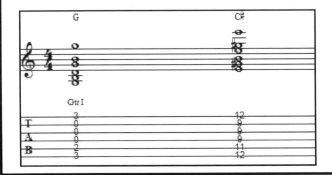
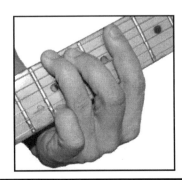

7C) UNLOCKING THE FRETBOARD - THE CAGED SYSTEM

4) Use the E shape and move it up nine semitones (*E - F - F# - G - G# - A - Bb - B - C - C#*)

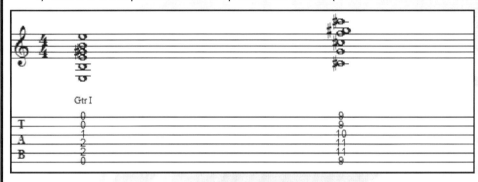

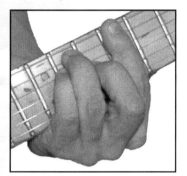

Here we are using the first finger to bar across the first fret and using the second, third and fourth fingers to from the E shape behind the bar.

5) Use the D shape and move it up eleven semitones *(D - Eb - E - F - F# - G - G# - A – Bb – B – C – C#)*

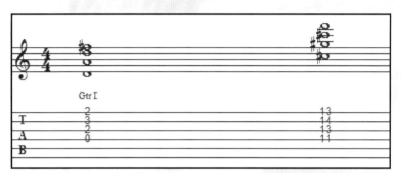

And what works with major chords will also work with their minor counterparts, although some of the shapes will be a little trickier physically so take these gently and don't overstrain your fingers!

1) Use the Cm shape and move it up one semitone (*C- C#*)

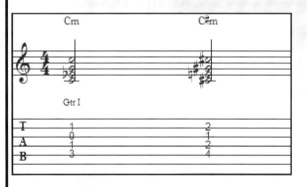

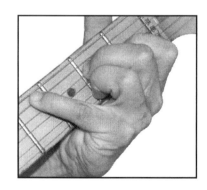

2) Use the Am shape and move it up four semitones (*A --Bb --B --C --C#*)

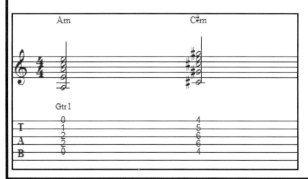

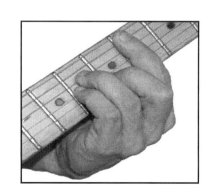

3) Use the Gm shape and move it up six semitones (*G - G# - A - Bb - B - C - C#*)

(Notice that in order to keep this shape physically playable I've omitted the notes on the B and E strings)

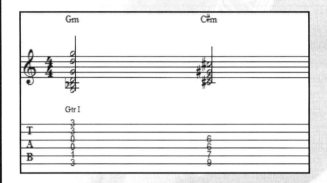
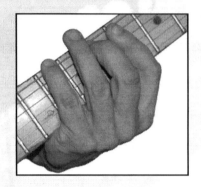

4) Use the Em shape and move it up nine semitones (*E - F - F# - G - G# - A - Bb - B - C - C#*)

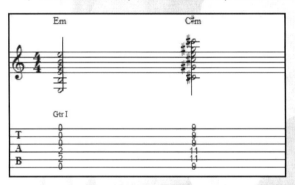
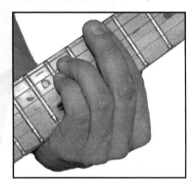

5) Use the Dm shape and move it up eleven semitones *(D - Eb - E - F - F# - G - G# - A – Bb – B – C – C#)*

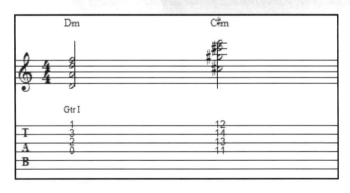
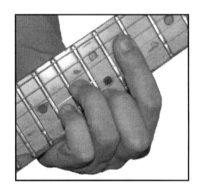

Now, try doing this for each of the twelve major and minor chords.

So.... now you have the knowledge and ability to play *every* major and *every* minor chord in five different places around the fretboard.

Pretty sweet. But we can do better still.

7C) UNLOCKING THE FRETBOARD - THE CAGED SYSTEM

THE MAJOR AND MINOR SCALES

A knowledge and understanding of the CAGED system gives us the ability to visualise the major and minor scales around the fretboard (also the associated modes of the major scale and the more exotic scales such as harmonic and melodic minor, but that is beyond the scope of this book).

I've deliberately shied away from dishing out bulky, unwieldy two-octave boxes for the major and minor scales, as they tend to be tricky to remember and difficult to use in practice. However, one octave patterns fall much more easily under the fingers and we can use these in conjunction with the CAGED system to help navigate the fretboard.

Laid out below are a set of easy-to-use one octave scale patterns that allow you to navigate the entire fretboard. For the sake of convenience I've tabbed them out in A, but practice them in every key. I would advise playing the chord shape, then the scale ascending, chord shape again, scale descending. This will really help to cement the relationship between chord shape and scale shape.

Relative to the major scale, the minor scale has a flattened 3rd, 6th and 7th intervals resulting in a mournful, melancholic sound:

A major scale	A	B	C#	D	E	F#	G#
	Root	2nd	3rd	4th	5th	6th	7th

A minor scale	A	B	C	D	E	F	G
	Root	2nd	flat 3rd	4th	5th	flat 6th	flat 7th

In the examples below, the chord tones are indicated in black with the non-chord scales tones in grey. In the accompanying audio examples, I will play the chord and then the scale fingering based on the chord shape.

1) A shape

AUDIO - TRACK 138

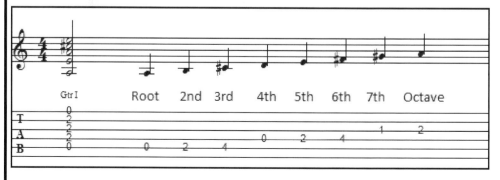

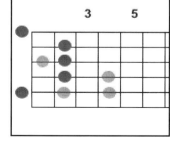

7C) UNLOCKING THE FRETBOARD - THE CAGED SYSTEM

A minor:

2) G shape:

Higher octave:

G minor:

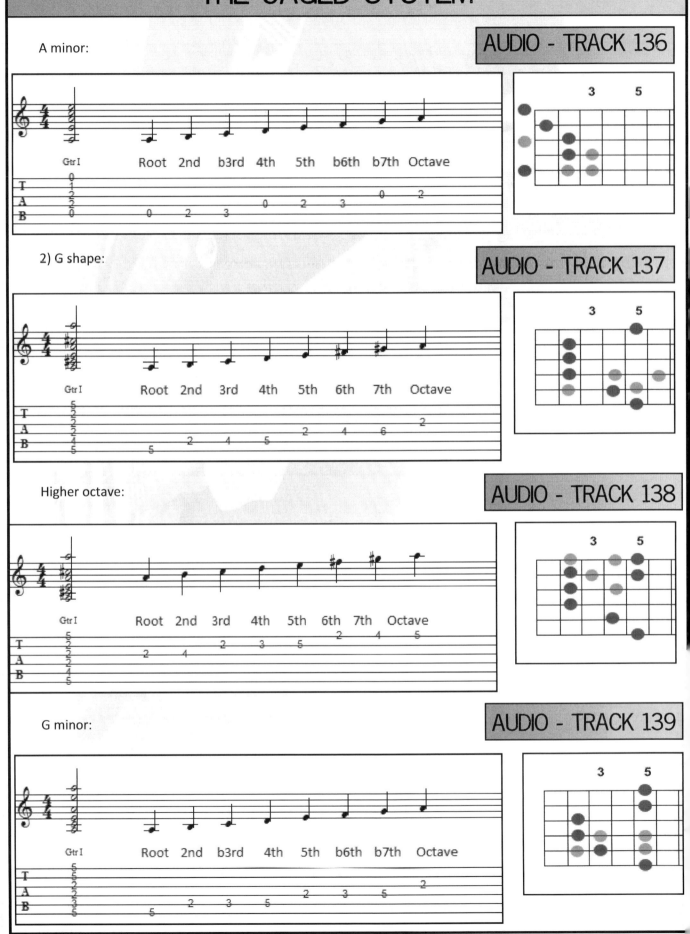

7C) UNLOCKING THE FRETBOARD - THE CAGED SYSTEM

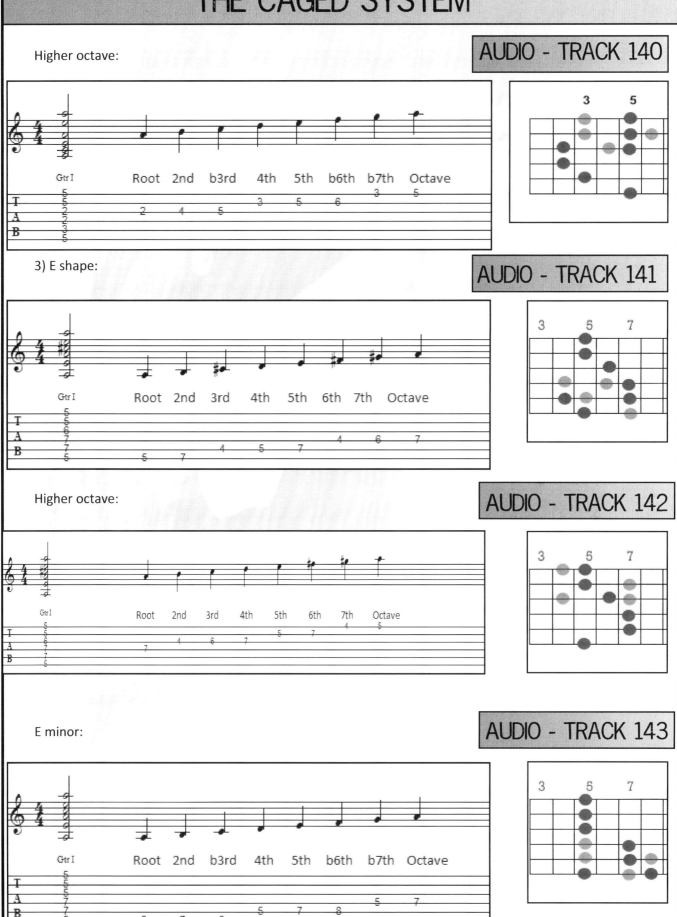

Higher octave:

AUDIO - TRACK 140

Gtr I — Root 2nd b3rd 4th 5th b6th b7th Octave

3) E shape:

AUDIO - TRACK 141

Gtr I — Root 2nd 3rd 4th 5th 6th 7th Octave

Higher octave:

AUDIO - TRACK 142

Gtr I — Root 2nd 3rd 4th 5th 6th 7th Octave

E minor:

AUDIO - TRACK 143

Gtr I — Root 2nd b3rd 4th 5th b6th b7th Octave

7C) UNLOCKING THE FRETBOARD - THE CAGED SYSTEM

Higher octave:

AUDIO - TRACK 144

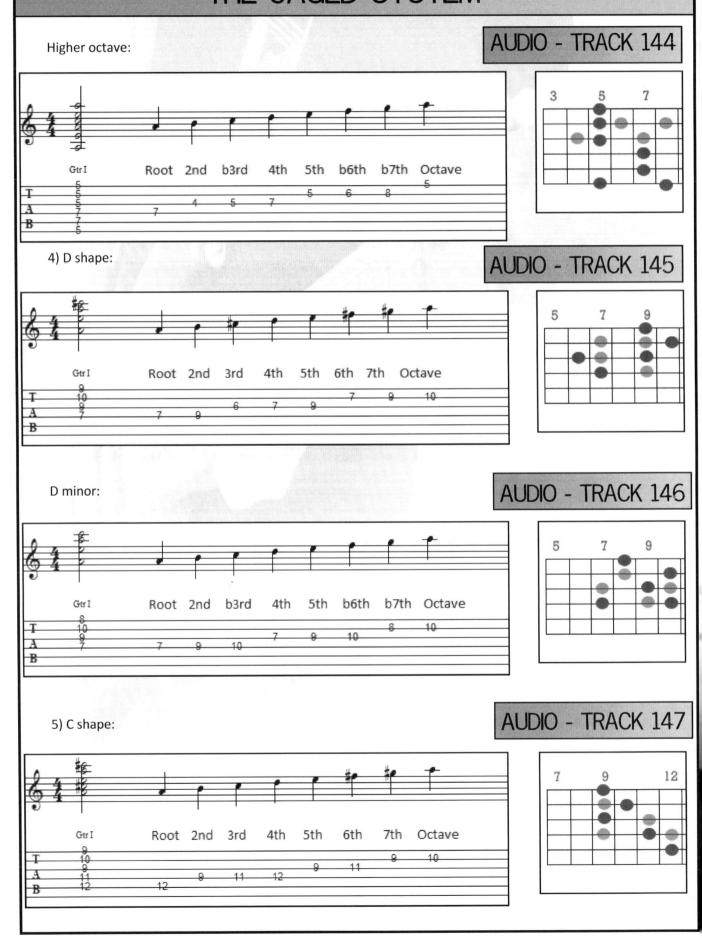

4) D shape:

AUDIO - TRACK 145

D minor:

AUDIO - TRACK 146

5) C shape:

AUDIO - TRACK 147

7C) UNLOCKING THE FRETBOARD - THE CAGED SYSTEM

C minor:

AUDIO - TRACK 148

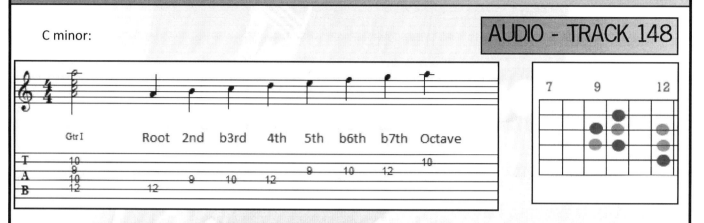

Practice improvising within these individual scale shapes, and then start linking them up - practice improvising within two shapes, then three, then four. Using the improvisation concepts outlined in Chapter 5, these shapes can help you to create melodic solo lines all over the neck. I've outlined a couple of examples below.

AUDIO - TRACK 149

BACKING - TRACK 150

AUDIO - TRACK 151

BACKING - TRACK 152

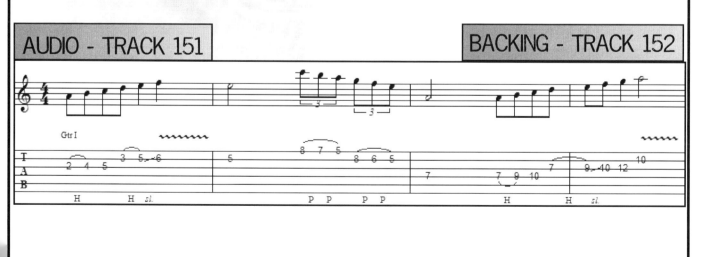

STAGE 7 PRACTICE ROUTINE

20 - 30 minutes per day:

1) Warm up (5 minutes):

AUDIO - TRACK 153

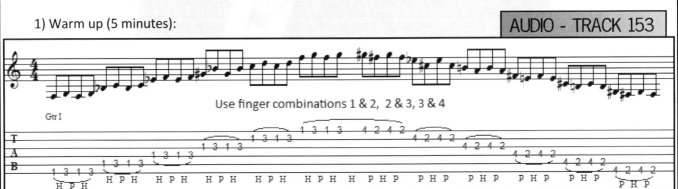

Use finger combinations 1 & 2, 2 & 3, 3 & 4

This legato exercise builds on the previous stage warm up but introduces an extra fret gap between the notes - use the first and second fingers across the first and third frets, first and third fingers across the first and fourth frets and stretching out to first and fourth fingers across the first and fifth frets. Essentially we're developing finger strength and independence, along with a smooth and even legato technique, while building reach and forcing your hand to find the absolute optimum thumb position for *you* - bearing in mind that this is always slightly different from player to player.

As before, set the tempo as low as you need to to play steady even eighth notes, and then begin to progressively speed up, using increments of 1 or 2 beats per minute (bpm). Once you've mastered the exercise, tweak it - try using a triplet rhythm.

2) New material (10-15 minutes): Repertoire,   (5- 10 minutes): Technical Development

Try and identify songs which build off the common chord sequences discussed in the section dealing with the Nashville Number System.

To give you some ideas:

I-V-vi-IV (D) - With Or Without You (U2)

I-vi-IV-V (A) - Stand By Me (Ben E. King)

Vi- IV- I - V (A) - Numb (Linkin Park)

Using the CAGED system will help you to figure out different ways to voice the chords, and using the scales will allow you to improvise melodically over the chord progressions

3) Warm down (5 minutes) : Improvisation

The "two bars on, two bars off" exercise discussed in the Stage 5 Practice routine is an excellent way to warm down as has already been mentioned, but there are a huge variety of backing tracks available, often for free. Apps like Session Band give you the ability to create your own by triggering loops, meaning you can tailor a specific chord sequence to improvise over. And failing that, there's always the radio - crank up and jam to whatever comes on!

STAGE 8: ROAD MAP: LEARNING TO LEARN

GOALS:

In this section of the book you will learn:

— *how to break down a song into sections*

— *how to recognise the key of a song*

— *how to use the ear and a basic knowledge of theory to identify frequently used generic chord sequences.*

— *how to arrange guitar parts based on simple chord sequences*

8A) OVERVIEW

The best approach to take when trying to learn a song or piece of music is the same as if you were attempting to draw a picture- getting the various objects in place (a house here, a person there, a bush in the corner) before filling in the details. I liken this approach to looking at a house: -if you look at a house from a distance you can clearly see that it's a house, where the windows and door are etc. However, as you get closer, the details come more into focus but it's no longer possible to see the entire house within your field of vision- you need to have the structure firmly imprinted in your mind's eye or the details won't make sense on their own. The closer you get, the more details reveal themselves but the harder it becomes to place them in context.

Most students, and unfortunately many teachers, start by cramming their faces right up against the brickwork- absorbing a great deal of detail but without any framework to place that detail in. This makes learning and remembering songs far more difficult than it needs to be and bypasses the basic cognitive skills of pattern recognition and information "grouping" - my method utilises those skills to their full. There's no magic involved, just a healthy dose of common sense, applied theory and a little bit of ear training – and the payoff is the ability to pick out a vast number of songs entirely by ear.

8B) STRUCTURE

The first thing to do with any song then, is to work out what the various pieces of the puzzle are and how to put them in order. In order to do this, we're going to need to work out where the verse changes to the chorus, to the bridge etc. This can be signalled by a musical cue such as a drum fill, a bass run, a particularly distinctive chord change, and it's also important not to underestimate the importance of vocal cues. If the vocalist sings a particularly distinctive lyric before each section change, that can also be a useful marker.

Many rock songs tend to follow a few standard structures:

a) Typical song structure

Intro

Verse

Bridge

Chorus

Verse

Bridge

Chorus

Solo

Chorus

b) More sophisticated variant

Introduction

Verse

Bridge

Chorus

Verse

Bridge

Chorus

Introduction/ Breakdown

Solo/ Middle 8

Chorus (often with key change)

8C) KEY

Finding the root, or tonic note is an essential part of finding your way through a song. This is one of the essential reference points that it's crucial to nail down so you can start deciphering the song you're trying to learn. Happily, there are only 12 notes, so barring studio trickery - occasionally recording studios would slightly speed up or slow down the the tape, resulting in a recording not tuned to concert pitch, and in older recordings bands would frequently tune using the studio piano as a reference point. Clearly, if the piano was not tuned to concert pitch, then the band wouldn't be either! These tricks occur rarely, but are not unknown, even on modern recordings.

NB- Be prepared to retune by ear if you really can't find the key.

The act of finding the key is a simple one – simply move through the chromatic scale until you find the note that feels like "home". Here are a few popular classic rock songs that you can use to help tune your ear in. I recommend playing the tonic note against the song to help train your ear to recognise the key.

Sweet Home Alabama – G

Sweet Child O' Mine – Gb

Back In Black – E

Sex On Fire – E

Johnny B Goode – Bb

Let's Stick Together – A

Here are a few pointers to help focus your efforts:

Rock/ blues/ punk songs tend to be in guitar-friendly keys such as A, E, D, G unless the band or artist tune down a semitone (as done by Hendrix, Guns 'n' Roses, and Stevie Ray Vaughan amongst others)

— Piano-led songs often favour keys that feature fewer sharp or flat notes like C, F, G, Bb, D.

— Songs that feature a lot of brass tend to favour keys such as Eb, Bb and Ab.

8D) HARMONY

Having deciphered the key, the next step is to work out the chord sequence for each section in turn. Many songs tend to be based around a relatively small number of standard chord progressions – put simply, there are only 12 notes, there are only a finite number of ways we can combine them, and more to the point, only a finite number of those combinations that actually sound good.

This is where an understanding of harmony and the Nashville Numbering System can make a huge difference – this was discussed at length in the previous chapter.

Firstly – do any of the chords sound out of place or "odd"? If yes, that means there are probably a few "accidentals" or *non-diatonic* chords, i.e. chords from outside the key. If not, however, that immediately narrows the field down to seven possible chords.

We can narrow that down a little more- do you hear the distinctive "horror movie" sound of the diminished chord? If not (and the chord is rarely used in popular music), that narrows the field further, down to six possible chords. Three major (the I, IV, and V), and three minor (the ii, iii and the vi, the relative minor).

Major and minor chords are easily identifiable – major sounds happy, minor sad. If all three chords sound happy, you're dealing with a I, IV, V or some variant thereof. All of a sudden we're down from "it could be any chord" to "It's these three chords, just figure the order".

Some examples :

– Twist & Shout / La Bamba – I, IV, V

– Knocking On Heaven's Door – I, V, IV

– Sweet Home Alabama – V, IV, I

– Lucky Man (The Verve) – IV, I, V

– Our old friend, the 12 bar blues - // I / I / I / I / IV / IV / I / I / V / IV / I / V //

Even these three chords can be identified by the role they play within the key – the I chord represents "home", the start and resolution of the musical journey. The IV, in its turn, represents a "lift" to the song while the V has a very definite tense character, pulling its way back to the I.

After the I, IV and V chords, the next most popular is the relative minor, the vi – some popular, well-used chord progressions are included below:

– Stand By Me / Every Breath You Take / Magic Moments – I, vi, IV, V

– Don't Stop Believin', When I Come Around, With Or Without You – I, V, vi, IV

– The Passenger, Africa, - vi, IV, I ,V

FINAL CUT

Your guitar can be your best friend.

Your guitar will do whatever you ask and respond to how you touch it. It has no ulterior motive, and asks nothing of you.

Your guitar will indulge and help you to express whatever emotion you can channel through it. Playing the guitar puts you in touch with a heritage of bards and minstrels that goes through thousands of years of human civilisation, tapping into a form of communication that predates and goes beyond language. The skills that you develop are yours, and yours alone to do whatever you want with, whether it's shredding your way through your own solo album or just strumming the odd Beatles song in the garden for the hell of it.

Your guitar – your voice.

Your rules.

Go play.

James Martin, 2015

www.jmguitartuition.co.uk

www.facebook.com/JMGuitarTuition

Twitter.com/jmguitartuition

jmguitartuitionuk@yahoo.co.uk

#0121 - 201016 - C0 - 297/210/6 - PB - DID1623061